Middle School

ON A WING AND A PRAYER

Coast-to-coast by ultralight across the US Bible Belt

To Bill Cheney,
with best wishes,

Colin

Colin MacKinnon
The Flying Scotsman

YORK HOUSE, EDINBURGH

First edition published by York House Publishing,
42 York Place,
Edinburgh, EH1 3HU

Published in the USA by Todd Huvard and Associates, Inc.
PO Box 25009,
Raleigh, North Carolina 27511-5009,

**A CIP catalogue record for this book
is available from the British Library.**

British edition:
ISBN 0 9532646 0 2

US edition:
ISBN 0-9622475-2-9

Jacket photographs and chapter headers by Richard Cook.
Graphics by Richard Palmer
Colour section photographs by author.

Printed in Great Britain
by TJ International, Padstow, Cornwall

Contents

For Marta,
who makes
my spirits soar
even when my
feet are firmly
on the ground.

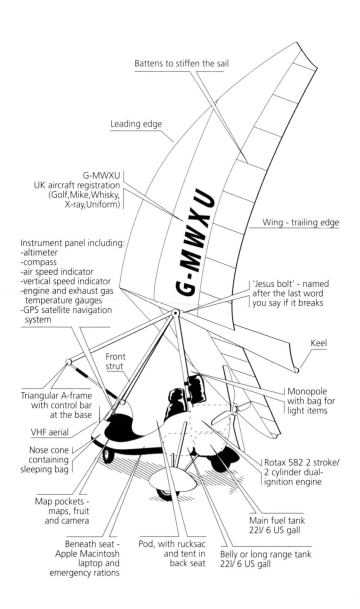

Battens to stiffen the sail

Leading edge

G-MWXU
UK aircraft registration
(Golf, Mike, Whisky,
X-ray, Uniform)

G-MWXU

Wing - trailing edge

Instrument panel including:
-altimeter
-compass
-air speed indicator
-vertical speed indicator
-engine and exhaust gas
 temperature gauges
-GPS satellite navigation
 system

'Jesus bolt' - named
after the last word
you say if it breaks

Keel

Front
strut

Triangular A-frame
with control bar
at the base

Monopole
with bag for
light items

VHF aerial

Nose cone
containing
sleeping bag

Rotax 582 2 stroke/
2 cylinder dual-
ignition engine

Map pockets -
maps, fruit
and camera

Main fuel tank
22l/ 6 US gall

Beneath seat -
Apple Macintosh
laptop and
emergency rations

Pod, with rucksac
and tent in
back seat

Belly or long range tank
22l/ 6 US gall

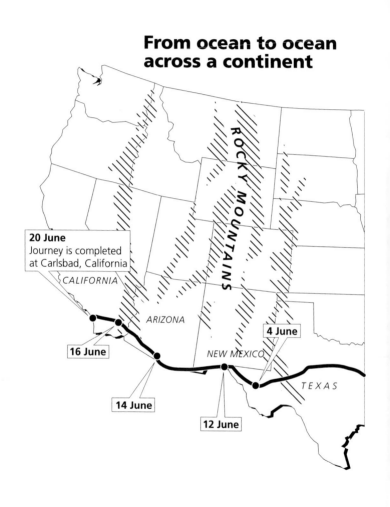

From ocean to ocean across a continent

ROCKY MOUNTAINS

20 June
Journey is completed at Carlsbad, California

CALIFORNIA

16 June

ARIZONA

14 June

NEW MEXICO

4 June

12 June

TEXAS

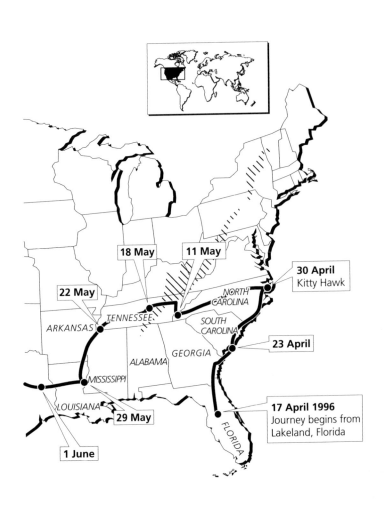

18 May

11 May

22 May

30 April
Kitty Hawk

NORTH CAROLINA

TENNESSEE

ARKANSAS

SOUTH CAROLINA

23 April

GEORGIA

ALABAMA

MISSISSIPPI

LOUISIANA

29 May

17 April 1996
Journey begins from
Lakeland, Florida

FLORIDA

1 June

Acknowledgements

Without Todd Huvard, publisher of the *Southern Aviator,* this flight would never have got off the ground. His gritty determination to overcome obstacles was an inspiration and the way his family accepted a total stranger into its midst gives new meaning to the word hospitality.

Thanks too, to Greg McGann for setting up a Web page during my travels. The e-mails it generated were a constant source of encouragement.

To Francis Rogallo, the inventor of the flexible delta wing that is the defining component of hang gliders and trikes, and to Mainair Sports, who have refined and developed it to produce world-beating aircraft, goes my unbounded gratitude.

Special thanks to Henri Bryan of Goretex, who provided my unique tartan flying suit, and to Lynx Micro for help with electronics.

My thanks also to Bill White and his flock in Anaheim, California, who entertained me at the end of my journey and helped return the Pink Panther to Scotland.

The airfield FBOs are unsung heroes. I salute your dedication.

Last, but not least, my thanks to the people of the South, where the traditional values of charm, courtesy and hospitality still flourish. You set a high standard for all of us to follow.

1

The Wright Stuff

*"The natural function of the wing is to soar
upwards and carry that which is heavy up to
the place where dwells the race of gods.
More than any other thing that pertains to the
body, it partakes of the divine."*

Plato, *Phaedrus*

One hundred years ago my Irish great-uncle covered himself in treacle and goose feathers, climbed a tree and leapt out, shouting: "Look at me! I can fly, I can fly!" So crazy attempts at flight are in my blood, and that was my excuse for setting off on a coast-to-coast flight across the United States from Kitty Hawk, North Carolina – where the Wright brothers made the world's first powered flight – to Long Beach, the end of the line for Calbraith Rodgers's first trans-continental flight.

The plan was simple: crate up my machine, fly it and myself over to the States, reassemble it and take off on an adventure through the history of flight. The US Federal Aviation Administration said that no airworthiness certificate was required for my aircraft and no licence was needed by ultralight pilots. So it really was going to be like those early days – happy-go-lucky red tape-free fun.

How wrong I was.

A week after I arrived in the US, my machine was still in England. Somehow, as the crated trike unit was being loaded into the aircraft someone smelled petrol. The consignment was immediately impounded by the Civil Aviation Authority as "dangerous cargo". Mainair, who had built my Flash II alpha five years ago and crated it up for the trip after an overhaul, were threatened with a fine of up to £4,000 (around $6,000) for failing to declare it as such. If the CAA could catch me, I would face a similar penalty.

After days of negotiations, the family putting me up in Raleigh, North Carolina, got a telephone call the day before Good Friday to say that if I didn't speak to someone in England within the next 20 minutes, it could be another two weeks before my aircraft could be shipped. Oh yes, there would also be a 50 per cent surcharge on the freight rate because my machine had become "dangerous".

I could not understand how there had been a problem. Both fuel tanks had been steam cleaned before the machine was delivered to Mainair, and I had watched them renew the fuel hoses before crating it up. Months later, I discovered that we had forgotten to clean out the carburetter bowls. When someone turned the crate upside down as they loaded it into the plane at Manchester, the equivalent of a teaspoonful of petrol must have dripped out. The $500 "dangerous cargo" surcharge makes that some of the most expensive fuel in the world!

The delays meant a change in plan. My thoughts had been to fly down the coast from Kitty Hawk to Florida, for Sun'n Fun, one of the largest airshows in the world and the biggest gathering of ultralight fliers. The trip down the coast would have been a shakedown flight and once at Sun'n Fun, Mainair's chief engineer, Roger Pattrick, would be able to give the aircraft a final check over. Now it seemed I would be lucky even to get the aircraft to the States before the show was over.

Cynthia Shelby, the freight company Emery Worldwide's agent at Raleigh-Durham airport, never once lost her patience with the frustrated flier in her office or the intransigent Brits across the Atlantic. For a week, it seemed she had devoted herself almost full time to tracking down what had happened to my aircraft. Within minutes, she was able to get the cargo diverted to Orlando, Florida.

It was time to redraw my plans. For months, sitting in the offices of *The Scotsman* newspaper in Edinburgh in the early hours of the morning, waiting for the first edition to come off the press, I had pored over maps and charts, dreaming of beaches and mountains, swamps and deserts; muttering under my breath as I rehearsed the correct phraseology for radio transmissions. As with the early pioneers, on both land and in the air, the Rocky Mountains loomed large in my thoughts; the final barrier to be overcome before the Pacific coast.

Out west, there seemed no choice. The further south one could go, the lower the mountains were. To the north, I faced a barrier 14,000ft high. While a Flash II alpha could handle that, I wasn't sure that I would be able to. In Britain, we are not allowed to fly above 10,000ft without oxygen. I was told that you can exceed that height in the United States – where everything, of course, is higher, smoother, faster – but as a cadet in the Royal Air Force I had undergone a high-altitude decompression in a hyper-baric chamber and experienced hypoxia. It was not something I wished to happen again if I was at the controls. A map of US airfields also showed some alarmingly large areas of white space to the north. Even to the south, the blue dots representing airfields were not exactly numerous. But the southern route was the one taken by pioneers like Cal Rogers, and despite Mainair's application of modern technology such as computer-aided design to the production of microlights (as ultralights are called in Britain), I felt that the old-fashioned priorities still applied.

In the east, my plan had been to fly down the coast to Florida, then skirt round the gulf to New Orleans, across Louisiana and into Texas.

Now I had to come up with a new route.

A visit to Kitty Hawk was a must. The final spur for my trip was a late night story on the Press Association wire service. The few paragraphs were based on a flowery press release by the auction house Sotheby's to promote a sale of aeronautica. What Simon, their press officer, did not expect was that his over-the-top sales pitch for a one-inch square piece of fabric from the original Wright Flyer, the world's first aircraft, would also launch another aviation adventure.

What price could be put on such a relic? I came up with a figure, decided to add the cost of a trip from Edinburgh to southern England and topped it off with the £200 I would earn in Glasgow that day by not travelling to the sale. Someone else was prepared to pay £1,500, but that was £100 less than my maximum. And I hadn't even seen what I was buying.

A fortnight later I collected a compact brown cardboard folder in London. Lot 91 included Christmas cards from childhood heroes such as Barnes Wallis, the inventor of the bouncing bomb that destroyed the Ruhr dams, and Douglas Bader, the legless Spitfire ace. Their bright colours had an instant appeal over the scruffy sheet of paper with its scrap of fabric attached. One card even suggested that the Wright Brothers' flights were not as historic as all that. On the front of Barnes Wallis's greeting sent from Vickers-Armstrongs was a picture of Ariel, a steam-driven monoplane designed by William Henson with John Stringfellow at Chard, Somerset, for which he was granted a patent in 1842. A printed note inside acknowledged: "Although Ariel was widely acclaimed, funds for its building were hard to come by; and when in 1847 a model was at last completed and tested, the result was a failure. Henson withdrew from the project; but Stringfellow continued the experiments and, in 1848, built a new model which became the first powered aircraft ever to fly."

The fabric had been saved by Lester D Gardner, a close friend of the Wrights, when the Kitty Hawk Flyer was being re-covered for display at the Massachusetts Institute of Technology. On Orville's death, Mr Gardiner sent out tiny scraps of "what I regard as the most valuable relic in aviation history" with the plea that the recipients should ensure in their wills that the fragments of fabric remain within the family "as Orville Wright would never have wanted it to be commercialized".

Oops, I thought. Sounds like I paid £1,600 for a big chunk of bad voodoo. But then an idea grew on me. Take this fragment back to Kitty Hawk for an open cockpit flight in its home air. Maybe it could create through my own machine a homeopathic aircraft, this tiny fragment embodying and transferring some of the the power and mystique of the original.

Whatever, it certainly brought me luck. The search for information on flying conditions at Kitty Hawk prompted me to send my first ever e-mail message. "You've hit the mother lode!" came the reply from Todd Huvard, former executive director of the First Flight Society and a board member. "I think you are about to embark on a grand adventure. How can I help."

After an exchange of e-mails in which we discussed his adventures flying in a Dakota to Normandy to drop some of the original D-Day paratroops on the 50th anniversary, and the address of the pub in Glasgow where they nightstopped and played petanque, Todd insisted I start the trip by getting the American Airlines direct flight from London Gatwick to Raleigh and stay with him and his family. It was an offer that saved my trip. Without Todd's help, I doubt if we would ever have sorted out the freighting tangle my machine got caught up in. His generosity with his time was all the more impressive considering he had to get the latest issue of his monthly magazine, the *Southern Aviator*, to bed and then gear up for the production of a daily newspaper at Sun'n Fun.

A fortnight after I arrived at Todd's, his brother-in-law, Travis, joked over dinner: "Do you think this guy really has got an aeroplane, or has he just come across a great way to get a free holiday?" But Cynthia had promised that my aircraft would be arriving in Orlando that Saturday. Travis was coming to Sun'n Fun and would be able to see it for himself.

2

High Noon

*"Skygod: being who reigns supreme while aloft
in a man-made flying contrivance, aeronautical
creature endowed with godlike attributes and
worthy in its estimation of human worship."*

Robert Gandt: *Skygods: The Fall of PanAm*

At last I was on route, albeit in Todd's Cessna 182. There was no question over who would sit in the left hand seat, the one reserved for the pilot in command. The question was, who would sit beside Todd – myself, who had a pilot's licence, albeit one for a microlight whose controls that work in precisely the opposite way to a standard aircraft, or Travis, who has a pretty fair idea of how to fly a Cessna after many hours as a passenger and suspected that the first time I had ever been in an aeroplane was on the way over the Atlantic.

It was close, but I got the front seat while Travis got the CD player. At 8,500ft, Todd handed me the controls and had a nap. Things went smoothly.

At a mile and a half high we were well above the early spring thermals. My gaze kept drifting towards the intra-coastal waterway and the Atlantic beaches which I should have been skimming down if everything had gone to plan.

After buzzing Todd's editor, Bill De Brauwer, as he drove the truck down to Florida, we called in to Walterboro to pick up some fuel. A marvelous character, Capt Ed Schaeffer, ran us down to a burger bar for lunch and entertained us with tales of his life as a PanAm pilot, finishing off on 747s.

Capt Ed was of the old school, the one that believes that out on the line all the girls are looking for husbands, and all the husbands are looking for girls. At least that's what I gathered when he said he had been married five times. His last wife was from his home town, Walterboro, so after being based all over the world, including Berlin where he married a German woman, of course, he was back where he started. "Great to see you guys," he said as we were leaving. "I'm only sorry I didn't come down to the field in my Rolls-Royce today. I could have given you all a ride in that."

At 500ft on the climbout, Todd told me: "You've got her." As I noticed the nose rising, I instinctively pulled back on the controls – only to see the horizon fall away even faster! It was the right movement for my microlight, but completely wrong for a three-axis aircraft. I corrected almost instantly, but not quickly enough for Todd not to notice (get the jitters?).

As I told Todd, it was a good illustration of why, in Britain, even an experienced 747 pilot like Capt Ed must do around six to eight hours of conversion training before being allowed to fly my type of machine. I also asked if he thought Capt Ed really had got a Rolls. "Hey, I wouldn't be surprised if he had one for each day of the week, and wives to go with them," Todd replied. "Do you know what those PanAm seven forty seven captains earned."

Approaching Florida, Todd got on the radio to request an air traffic advisory. A torrent of words came pouring back. All I could think was: "Well, I'll have to keep away from controlled airspace if they all talk like this." Todd was unshaken. "You ... all ... hear ... the ... speed ... at ... which ... I ... talk," he transmitted. "Wey...ull, ... that ... is ... the ... speed ... at ... which ... I ... think. Please say again."

I mentioned my doubts. "Just don't take any sh** from controllers," he replied. "Remember, you are in charge of the aircraft. You are the one responsible for safety. They are on the ground, you are in the air. It is always your call."

As we approached Lakeland, the airfield looked little different from many others across the States, three big runways – although only two seemed to be in use now – and a cluster of hangars around the apron to the north.

Two days later, you couldn't move for aircraft – there must have been more aeroplanes at that one field than there are on the entire British register. And if a space didn't have an aircraft parked on it, someone had pitched a tent there.

Acclimatising to the heat and the sheer scale of Sun'n Fun took me days. At first, I thought it unfair that ultralights had their own grass strip on the southern boundary. Then I saw general aviation aircraft landing three at a time on the main runway. I had never experienced anything on this scale. Every type of aircraft imaginable was there, from a jet-powered microlight to enough privately owned warbirds to re-enact a Korean War dogfight.

True to Cynthia's word, my microlight was ready to be collected from Orlando on the Saturday. Yes, the "Pink Panther", as it had become nicknamed, had finally made it to America. The delays had been frustrating, but starting at Sun'n Fun had the advantage of getting the machine uncrated and re-assembled in the company of experts.

I had bought G-MWXU from a friend, Gerry Doughty, at the East of Scotland Microlight Club. Gerry owned a Flash II alpha with a 582cc Rotax engine, the exact model I had decided to use, and had wanted to join me on my adventure but couldn't raise the funds. Then he sold me his machine and used my cash to invite himself along for a fortnight.

The original plan had been to spend the first week at Sun'n Fun and then take a week to fly down to Key West and back. Because of the weight limits, I was going to leave all my equipment at Lakeland and collect it when I dropped Gerry off for his fight home. The new plan was to leave my gear with Todd and collect it in Raleigh after flying up to Kitty Hawk with Gerry in the back.

At Mainair's factory in Lancashire, England, Jim Cunnliffe and his crew had a fully-equipped facility to help disassembe the Pink Beast, as they called it, and crate it up. Gerry and I had much more limited equipment, just a couple of 5/16th and 7/16th inch spanners – which Roger Patrick, Mainair's chief engineer, said would fit just about everything on the airframe – the wooden crate and an open field. As the temperature rose into the 80s, we also found we had a very limited vocabulary!

To raise the trike to fit the rear undercarriage we rigged up a hoist using pieces of the crate. Even then, it was no easy task ... the air was blue before we finished, partly because notes I had made in Rochdale did not cover how washers should be fitted where the drag link from the rear wheels connected to the keel. Fortunately, so we thought, a chap called Tony appeared and said he had once distributed Mainair machines in the US and knew the correct order for the various parts.

Next day, Roger from Mainair turned up and looked over the machine. The only thing he said we'd got wrong was the way the washers were fitted! So it was another couple of hours in the sun – no fun – to put that right.

One thing that surprised Gerry and I was just how flimsy many US ultralights were. One flier parked his floatplane next to ours and I swear there was not an aluminium tube on it as thick as the thinnest component on the Pink Panther.

I asked its owner about a badly bent tube that ran along one side of the keel and he said it had got crunched as he was loading the machine on to his truck. He had tried to straighten out the one on the other side, but it had broken as he pulled on it.

I had always fancied flying a floatplane, but not this one. The next day a small storm came through and the following morning the wing of his aircraft was just a heap of twisted metal and fabric.

The ultralighters at Sun'n Fun have nicknamed their area Paradise City. Squelch through it after a cloudburst and you'll understand why. For my maiden flight in America, Todd talked the ultralight airshow's veteran commentator, Vernon Peckham, into allowing me to appear during the midday manufacturer's showcase.

It was high noon, literally and metaphorically.

I hadn't flown since February 26, when I took the newly-acquired Pink Panther for a shake-down flight from East Fortune, near Edinburgh, Scotland, for a 1 hour 40 minute flight to Eshott, outside Newcastle, England. On that trip the throttle cable froze open as I descended to cross the English border and I had to tell my passenger, a fellow microlighter, James Neil, that we might have to divert to a nearby airfield, circle over it and then shut the engine down for a dead-stick landing. As it happened, I was able to pull on speed and bring us down at 50-100 ft per minute until the warmer air nearer the ground unfroze the cable.

This time there would be no such problems, the perspiration was pouring off me – and it was not just the heat.

A five-minute trip round the circuit and I was coming in to land. I should have held the flare a little longer to make a better landing but the crowd were happy. As I rolled to a halt, I could hear their applause. At last, Todd had seen my aircraft fly.

I only flew a couple more times at Lakeland; once to take Gerry up and once with Arnold Greenwell, who was taking photographs for Todd's airshow newspaper, *Sun'n Fun Today*. Gerry and I agreed that the airspace was just too crowded for us. The circuit height was limited to 500ft and trying to keep to what I would regard as a safe separation distance seemed impossible with ultralights taking off every 15 to 20 seconds.

There was also the extra "attraction" of powered parachutes cluttering up the airspace. When I thought how they seemed to us that they just get in the way, I realised just how we, in turn, must appear to larger general aviation aircraft.

Things all worked out smoothly, though. The great thing about Sun'n Fun is the people. As well as the thousands of unsung heroes who work for months to prepare the site and the entertainment programme, there were also the aircraft designers and fliers from all around the world.

A highlight for me was to meet Joe Kittinger. In 1960, before I was born, he went up in a helium balloon to 108,000ft, jumped out to freefall for 4min 36sec – passing through the sound barrier at 90,000ft going at around 714mph before the air got thick enough to slow him down. Asked what his wife thought about all this derring-do, he looked over to the young woman operating the slide projector and smiled: "She wasn't even born then!"

A night pyrotechnic and aerobatic display ended Sun'n Fun for me – a good send off. Don't let anyone who flies with lit explosives strapped to their aircraft say I'm crazy.

As Gerry and I pre-flighted the Pink Panther, our new friends gathered to wish us luck. It was a nervous moment. The start of a big adventure, three months of flying to unknown airfields, unsure of the local quirks in the air, uncertain of the welcome.

As I was running through the check list, Tony turned up and insisted on asking question after question as I was trying to complete my airframe examination. I was close to losing my temper, and told Gerry: "OK, let's just get out of here."

As ultralights, we had a five-mile corridor to the south, with a 500ft ceiling, for our exit route from the zone around Lakeland. I had bought a GPS satellite positioning unit to help with the navigation, choosing the same model that Gerry had so that he could teach me how to use it. With difficulty, we programmed in the route to take us south from Lakeland and then west and to the north.

Five miles south and I realised the GPS was telling us to head east, instead of west. We were off the edge of the map – I had thought, another error, that since we'd be just skirting Lakeland there was no need to shell out $12 on another sectional – so I decided to drop into a large field so we could reprogramme the GPS.

Turning back to Lakeland was not an option because the exclusion zone for the afternoon airshow was about to take effect.

"I thought you said this was the model you owned, how come we've got the wrong stuff in it?" I asked Gerry. "I thought you'd used all this before?"

"Ah, um, well ..." he replied. "You see, back home I get Phil to put all the stuff in it. He's the one who really knows all about these things."

A farmer had spotted us coming down and asked whether we need help. We explained things as a problem with our computer – always blame a machine! – and let his son sit in the Pink Panther and hold the control bar while we had a chat. Almost immediately the subject of God came up.

The farmer was the first of many deeply-religious people I was to meet. I do not attend any particular church but I am always surprised to find fliers who do not feel a sense of awe about being in the air. Man can swim across water to avoid using a boat and walk to cover ground without a car. But without an aircraft, or balloon, or kite, we cannot fly. And however scientifically we examine the air, there are always hidden little surprises.

Roger Bacon, a 13th century Franciscan friar, had his own views on this. "It is not necessarily impossible for human beings to fly, but it so happens that God did not give them the knowledge of how to do it. It follows therefore that anyone who claims that he can fly must have sought the aid of the devil. To attempt to fly is therefore sinful."

As we prepared to leave, the farmer wished us God speed and asked if we would mind them saying a prayer for us. After strapping in, I looked round before shouting "Clear prop!" to find him and his wife and their four children kneeling on the grass with their hands clasped.

3

Coasting Along

*"The course of the flight up and down was
exceedingly erratic, partly due to the
irregularity of the air, and partly to lack of
experience in handling this machine"*

Orville Wright, on the Wright Flyer

A few minutes later we were back on course and Gerry was preparing to say his own prayers. As we headed north we were well aware that we would be passing under the what would be long finals for zero-nine, the active runway at Lakeland so decided to keep at 500ft to make sure we were right out of the way. The eastern fringes of Plant City stretched out in front of us, and flying around it and the zone around its airfield was more than I could bear, so I kept on track.

Gerry wanted to know what we'd do if the engine failed. We were both pretty uncomfortable at being forced into an awkward position. And it was getting pretty bumpy as the day's heat built up.

When I suggested we could always land on a factory roof, Gerry accused me of being a maniac. As a joiner, he knows the dangers of roofs. Falling off, or through, roofs is one of the perils of his trade. My thought was that even if the trike went through, the wing would hold us suspended over the factory floor. We didn't have to test the theory!

Just half an hour into the trip and we were both edgy; the air is rough and my arms were getting tired. Chewing steaks and lifting little cans of American beer over the past week hadn't given me very much exercise.

A few miles north of the city there was a nice big field, so we decided to put down until the day cooled a little. First attempt I was a bit high, so we went around for a second try. Still a bit high but I decided I am getting it down. As I pulled on speed to dive off the height, Gerry started to get really nervous. As we touched down – quite long – he shouted "go around, go around". By now, I've decided we are down and that's that. Gerry screams about the fence ahead, but we stop 20-30 yards short. Unlike Gerry, I am used to an old Flash I, which just has a metal bar to press against the front wheel for a brake, so I know all the other tricks. Gerry says we were lucky, I give him the old reply that I'd rather be lucky than good, and add that if we are what we eat, he should eat less chicken.

An hour later, we were hot and bored so decided to head to the next airfield, Zepherhills. Just as we kitted up, a helicopter appeared with the local sheriff. An engineer on a passing train reported an aircraft in a field and wondered if it was in any difficulty. Gerry thought it was amusing following my landing – I reminded him that a good landing is one you walk away from. Well into the aviation cliche game, he replies: "And a 'great' one is when you can use the aircraft another time."

Back in the air, it was only a dozen or so miles to Zepherhills. Minutes after take-off, we passed over an unmarked grass strip with a flex-wing trike on the flightline. If only we had realised it was one of just four other Mainair machines in the States.

On the ground at Zepherhills, a friendly guy at the FBO showed me how to refuel by swiping my credit card through the pump to start it. It was the first time I had seen such technology at an airfield. The other side of the field was a parachute school and cafe, so a quick taxi took us to lunch.

A parachutist in his fifties rushed over as we switched off and shouted: "Hey, I've got one of those! Where'you from?"

We thought we had met a fellow trike pilot, but then he explained that he also owned a Mainair Flash II alpha. It was his machine we had flown over a few minutes earlier.

Dave told us he had bought his trike after seeing an alpha at Sun'n Fun a few years earlier and had since modified it somewhat. He had taken a few lessons from Tony but felt he wasn't really learning anything so taught himself to fly – this is the land of the free, everyone kept telling me.

One of his modifications sounded interesting; he had attached winglets, which he claimed was now being done by hang-gliders and gave him an increased climb rate and decreased fuel consumption, due to the reduction in wingtip vortexes.

The other thing he had done was to weld a step on the undercarriage for parachutists. When I said he must be pretty good at dead stick landings by now, he replied that he didn't kill the engine before they stepped off.

Dave was surprised at the warmth of our welcome from the FBO – he'd been banned after taking parachutists up in his alpha. I was not surprised. I couldn't work out was who was crazier: him for letting them jump with his engine still running, or them for jumping out in front of a spinning propeller.

It's not an unreal danger. Within a month I was to meet a man who had had a hand caught in a prop and see a dog getting its shoulder sliced open when an engine started. The only fault I found on the Pink Panther after its first flight at Sun'n Fun was a short in the engine electrics, which meant the engine wouldn't stop when the magneto switches were flicked off. The technical reason for this is that unlike ordinary switches, these ones work in reverse by shorting the circuit when in the on position. So all the time Gerry had been hand-swinging a "dead" prop to suck fuel through, the engine had been ready to fire and take a careless finger off.

Fed and watered, we took off in the evening for Crystal River. Yes, we were meant to be heading east towards the Atlantic coast and it is on the Gulf of Mexico, but two old timers at Zepherhills said it was very pretty, so we thought: "What the heck!"

The two men were in the tradition of Captain Ed, and when they heard we had to have licences to fly microlights in the UK one of them produced his old British licence from the early 1950s, before trikes had been invented. He had flown a lot in Africa and had acquired a British licence so he could fly British aircraft in any of our former colonies. He was up for a flight in the Pink Panther, but, rather than tell him we thought he was too frail, I pointed out that he didn't have the right rating on his British licence!

We, in turn, showed him our licences which are like a small book, yet don't have space for a photograph – unlike the current US licences which resemble credit cards.

At Crystal River, we arrived at dusk just as the FBO was locking up, but he recommended a cheap motel – which turned out to share its front desk with a Bible bookshop – before rushing off. We thought his welcome a bit abrupt, but reckoned it was Saturday night so he had other things on his mind. I later found out just how hard FBOs work, so it made it all the more surprising when we turned up at 7:30 the next morning to discover they had hoisted a Union Jack in our honour on one of their flagpoles.

The ride to Williston was pretty, with the morning light shining on the low lying ground. We never really got to see Crystal River in the daylight. The air seemed to get quite bumpy early on, so we stayed at Williston for the day, getting a lift into town for lunch in what we would consider a typical US cafe/restaurant, one busy waitress serving about a dozen tables and still finding time for a pleasant word with everyone. We just beat the rush of people from the church across the road and later watched the waitress stand in embarrassment holding two hot plates of food as the preacher and his daughter said what felt like the longest Grace you could imagine.

The evening flight east took us to Palatka. My target was St Augustine, thus crossing Florida from west to east in a day, but as it grew darker it was obvious we might only just make it by nightfall. Looking at the light winds, I decided to land on the north-south runway. As I transmitted that I was on short finals for three-five, a lady in a Cessna called out that she was taking off from zero-nine, the east/west runway and that it was the active one. Without thinking – other than to avoid any smash at the intersection, since I had been planning to land long because the FBO was at the far end of the runway – I replied that I would abort my approach and follow in behind her.

As I turned away I realised she had taken off directly downwind, but then thought: "What the heck, it's only a 5-8mph tailwind and this runway is more than 5,000ft long, so if I can't get the Pink Panther down before the end of it I'll never be able to show my face back at East Fortune (where we have just hundreds of feet of concrete) again."

As we taxied up to the FBO, the lady announced that they were closing, that there was no taxi service on a Sunday and she did not know where the nearest motel was. A plane load of parachutists had just gone up, so we could wait and try our luck with them.

"You the guys that just landed downwind?" the the jump plane pilot asked. "Yes, there was some woman who said it was the active runway and took off on it," I replied. "Oh that was just crazy Annie," you should have ignored her," he replied. A little local knowledge is a useful thing, I thought, although a bit late this time.

Outside our motel we felt like obvious tourists, being the only white faces around, so it was with some trepidation we decided to walk back to the airfield the next morning – Palatka being short on taxis early in the morning too.

But only a few minutes along the road a black guy on his way home from work pulled over and offered us a lift to the airfield. "Just doing my Christian duty," was his reply to our thanks.

Good people are good people the world over but I am not in any rush to revisit Palatka. Neither is Todd, it turns out. On the way back from Sun'n Fun he was overhead Palatka at the correct altitude for his heading when a Mooney went shooting past him head on and just 20ft below. Maybe it was Crazy Annie.

Some pilots say we had priority since we were on finals and so should have landed. My attitude is that if someone is daft enough to do a downwind take-off like that, I'm not going to rely on them allowing me to land in front of them. If they cannot see the windsock, they will probably not spot me either. Next time, though, I'll do a go-around and come back to my original choice.

Anyway, we cut around the top of the controlled airspace at St Augustine – thus missing the oldest city in the US and its star-shaped fort – to catch the coast and refuel at Fernandina. Posters on the wall showed us the tourist sights we missed.

At Maryport, there was a huge carrier group tied up in the dock – we counted 17 ships and a carrier with a deck the size of a small town. Looking at that empty expanse, the temptation was almost overwhelming, if only to boast to an old friend of mine in London, James White, who used to tell of the time he was on a Swordfish which landed across, instead of along, the deck of an American carrier in Hong Kong harbour.

By now, we had the beginnings of a good tailwind, something we were really going to enjoy tomorrow. At St Simons Island, Georgia, we made the first of my "must do" stops. When I saw the name on the chart – McKinnon Field – I knew I just had to visit. A reply to a letter to Glynn County regional library in Brunswick a few months before I left told me that Malcolm Baker McKinnon had been born there in 1882 and eventually became mayor. After a successful career as a broker he set up the McKinnon Oil Company in 1928. He must have had canny Scots blood somewhere in his lineage to switch out of broking the year before the Wall Street crash.

Larry Wade and his staff were wonderful, giving myself and Gerry a car so we could have a day on the beach. After lunch at the Mullet Head bar/restaurant we chilled out and lazed around in the sun. And when we revisited the Mullet Head for a Coke before going back to McKinnon field they refused to charge us since we had eaten there earlier in the day. That seemed to sum up the friendly spirit of a place where people still have the time to remember a face. My memory was not so good. Just after take-off I realised I had forgotten to take that essential picture of myself in my tartan Goretex suit next to the airfield sign.

Another unusual person we met was Bill Walker, who has spent his life making and losing money on cars, trucks and planes. His latest venture was helping to build a new airline in Lithuania from the remains of Aeroflot's local operations and that led him to import 11 rugged Antonov An-2s, the famous Flying Truck biplanes built in the 1980s to a 50-year-old design. They made a striking sight at the airfield.

I had called Hilton Head to check that the US Masters had finished and we would be able to get somewhere to stay. The 90-mile flight took us just under two hours, and feeling more confident about ourselves and our machine we larked about, dropping down to buzz along some of the beaches for a while before climbing to ensure a safe height for the many water crossings.

Although we had missed the golfers by a day, the big city prices remained. We ate in a McDonalds, had a beer at the motel and hit the hay. It had been a long day and the forecast for the morning was good: strong winds but in the right direction. Once we had paid our bill, the motel where we had stayed suddenly became somewhat reluctant to run us back to the airfield. So we called a cab instead. For a $10 fare, it didn't seem very far – and all the corners seemed to have been left turns. We taxied to the north and took off heading south, only to see the last building on our left was the FBO where we had left the Pink Panther for the night with, just beyond the fence, the motel. Taxis $10: Tourists 0.

The two guys on the line that morning had asked if we'd seen the film *Braveheart*, adding: "Hey, it's like yo Scots are jes same as us. Y'all were really rolled over by them English."

The cab driver must have been a yankee carpetbagger. Still, a 79mph groundspeed with just 45mph airspeed made up for a lot. On take-off, the plan was to orbit the field for a few minutes to pick up enough height for the sea crossing north across Port Royal Sound. The strong tailwind, however, made a neat circle almost impossible, so I just turned for the coast, then headed south, or tried to – with the headwind I was almost stationary and just climbing like a rocket.

At 2,000ft, it was due north and up the coast for Georgetown. The massive tailwind meant the five-mile crossing of Port Royal Sound was almost over before I could worry. Fifteen miles north, St Helena Sound was even wider, but with the strong tailwind there would be no dithering about which shore to head for if the engine went pop. I just fixed my eyes on the far beach and went for it.

We kept clear of the Charlestown zone by following the intra-coastal waterway and watched the groundspeed hit 79mph, and that was throttling back and pushing the bar out nearer the stall to lower the airspeed to less than 45mph. By now we were beginning to get a little worried about the landing at Georgetown, with wind like this at just 1,500ft. I wanted to go lower but the coast is so broken up it was impossible to follow the beach, and rather than climb and descend all the time to cross the water, I kept between 1,500 and 3,000ft. Some of the inlets and islands looked pretty remote.

Cutting inland after Bull Island, it was straight along the highway to Georgetown – three runways in the old wartime pattern. We were at 500ft over the end of the concrete on runway two-nine and I landed at the start of the numbers and was stopped before the paint finished, a straight down descent!

My mother had visited Georgetown a few years ago and said its old architecture shouldn't be missed. Strangely, the moment we landed at the airfield, I felt uneasy about the place. Despite the large runways, there was a rundown, no-one cares atmosphere about the place. Just a couple of hangers, looking neglected rather than that tatty well-worn look you get when people are too busy to give things a coat of paint just yet – the I'll do it tomorrow, you know, syndrome! The dozen or so aircraft tied down also looked as though they'd never flown for months.

Inside, despite our strange bird and my tartan plumage, the lady at the counter never batted an eye or offered any help. It was obvious from the forecast we were spending the night here, so it was off with the wing and and we got the whole thing tied down in a hollow under some trees. One of those massive thunderstorms we had been warned about was due, so no chances were being taken.

A taxi took us into a motel in town and we went for a swim in the pool (we were the first people to do so that year, the water that was still too cold for Americans was just right for Scots) and then ate as much as we could for five bucks at a cafeteria called Quincy's across the road. It was my first experience of American all-you-can-eat buffets. Gerry and I thought our waitress Tina was being paid by the amount we ate she was so determined to fill up our plates.

With 110 miles flown in 95 minutes that morning, we felt pretty pleased with ourselves. Unfortunately there was not much in the way of nightlife to help us celebrate; we were the only people in two of the town's bars, in the third one, on the boardwalk, we were thrown out because it was for members only ... it, of course, was the only bar with customers.

On he way back to the motel, we saw some flashes of lightening, so the forecast thunderstorms were putting in an appearance after all. There was a lot of wind too, and the gale was still blowing in the morning. We took all our clothes – apart from swimming trunks – and put them in the washing machine while we sat by the pool, to be eaten alive by the gnats. No-one had warned us, so since we had checked out of our rooms, it was a 60-minute swim until our clothes were clean and dry.

Back at the airfield that afternoon, clean and refreshed and culturally enriched by a stroll around the historic houses of South Carolina's third oldest port, we popped the wing back on the Pink Panther, loaded up, refuelled and headed off. Not a word from the airfield manager who sat in his office with the door open as we settled up for fuel.

According to the chart, as long as we kept above 2,500ft going past Myrtle Beach we were clear of their airspace. It was a bit unnerving, nevertheless, to find commercial jets taking off down the runway and pass less than 1,000ft below.

After one crossed about a mile in front of us, I decided to pull the bar in and stuff my foot down on the throttle when I saw another taxiing for take-off. Somehow, it didn't seem so bad when it passed a mile or so behind us – at least, not so bad if you kept looking ahead.

We popped down at Ocean Isle and chatted to a few folk who said accommodation would be a lot easier at Southport, so it was back in the air for a 30-minute hop. The airfield office at Brunswick County was shut by the time we got there at 8pm, so we tied down the aircraft and strolled down to the main road, pausing for a quick photocall at the sign, Brunswick County Airport, North Carolina _ we had made it to the First Flight State.

Gerry said go left, I said go right, the map has the town marked that way. He insisted we should go left, so we did. Go with the flow, I say. I had been navigating in the air – very difficult, just keep the sea on the right hand side – so decided he could navigate on the ground. All I wanted was food and a bed. Hey, we were in the Kitty Hawk state, the Wright Brothers' air, it was time to celebrate – neither of us really thought we would get this far when we set out from Sun'n Fun and we had now flown in four of the United States.

It was two miles before we found a restaurant. As much seafood as we could eat for six bucks. We ate a lot. Gerry showed the waitress our scrap of the Wright Flyer, since we were in North Carolina, and it turned out that she and her sister owned the restaurant and her sis was a pilot. Strangely, the relic impressed the waitress more than it did her sister. Or maybe it was just Gerry's dark good looks.

The girls offered us a lift to the nearest motel, "it's only just up the road", but we decided to walk off our blowout. Another two miles and we were at roach motel. Lesson number one about America: nobody walks anywhere, so they don't know how far away places are. Or that, when it is dark, you can't see holes dug in the grass verge by the road.

Next morning, a bright and early dawn flight had been the plan. A four-mile walk put paid to that. At the airfield, we were getting ready to go when Heather Sherfinski arrived to open up. As we refuelled, she raved about our machine. So: "Fancy a flight?" asks Gerry. A quick trip around Southport enabled her to point out to him all the restaurants and good motels that were just a mile to the right when one leaves the airfield!

It was the first time in seven months Heather had been flying, and she works at an airfield. So don't assume airfield staff get free flights all the time. Make their day, offer to take them up.

Before she took up Gerry's offer, Heather telephoned her boss Howie Franklin to ask (plead?) if it was OK to shut up the office for ten minutes while she went for a fly, but she only called her husband afterwards in case he thought an ultralight was too dangerous.

Little did she know, but this was to turn out the scariest day of my trip, leaving me feeling as though I had cheated death three times. Boy did I need a beer when I got to Beaufort, NC, that night.

4

Life's A Beach

"In the development of air power, one has to look ahead and not backward and figure out what is going to happen, not too much what has happened."

Brig Gen "Billy" Mitchell

At Bradley Aviation on St Simons Island I had had a new rectifier wired in to power a charger for the radio and headsets, but I had never really had a chance to see whether it worked. At most of the airfields I visited you just transmit blind on the Unicom frequency for other traffic to hear, but a couple of times I had been having problems requesting weather and traffic advisories, although my reception was perfect. At Georgetown I suspected that we had just been ignored, at Southport the office was unmanned when we arrived. A radio check on the ground before we left worked fine, however.

As we flew up the coast we faced the only piece of restricted airspace on the whole coastal trip, a

20-mile long box between Camp Lejeune and the Atlantic.

Calls to the Marine Corps at Cherry Point went unanswered. There seemed little choice, we had to get through somehow. The alternative was to go inland, but with all the restricted zones in the area the only way back to the Outer Banks was a 25-mile crossing over Pamlico Sound – that's further over water than the shortest crossing of the English Channel, and with a dodgy radio ....

As the zone approached, we still hadn't decided and even over the coast the air was getting hot and rough. Gerry felt like buzzing the beach, we'd got a good tailwind and would be through the 20 miles in just over 15 minutes. An airstrip was marked on the chart at Topsail Island, so I decided to seek it out and drop in there for the afternoon so we could work things out. Maybe get local advice.

As we flew around, the field was not very obvious. "Look, what's that here," Gerry said, pointing to not just one but two abandoned airfields with a couple of huge weed-covered runways each. Perfect. I couldn't believe our luck. It was all a bit strange, though. The runways were not even marked on our sectional as "disused but useful for navigation". We double checked our navigation: "Which side was the sea on, which side was the land?"

Yes, we were heading north. Yes, we had flown over Topsail Beach and Surf City. Yes, we hadn't reached the restricted area. Great, this will do nicely, I thought.

On finals, 50ft off the ground, Gerry said: "F***". At the same time, my peripheral vision registered that there was something wrong with the bushes by the runway. As I thought "well, it's too late, I'm landing anyway, the runway is clear" my mind began to work out that the place was swarming with troops in full camouflage.

We got down and taxied over to the abandoned apron. Gerry and I checked that we were both seeing the same thing ... field guns wrapped in camouflage netting, troops, Jeeps. Everywhere.

"Take off, take off, let's get the heck out of here," urged Gerry.

"They're trained killers, they've got our number," I replied.

"I told you, we should just have flown up the beach at 100ft, now look what you've down," he answered back.

"Shut up, I'm thinking... look, we've got a problem with the engine, we've made a precautionary landing, They can't do anything to us for that. You're always allowed to make a precautionary landing anywhere. Maybe we are in the restricted area, but it must be only just. If we *are* in it, we just need to say that we were outside it when we got in trouble so we made for the nearest spot, right here. Now get out and start fixing the engine. Remember, that cylinder-head temp gauge has never worked, let's check it out. Come on, get a screwdriver and pretend to be doing something, they'll be watching us with their telescopic sights. I'll do the talking."

A few minutes later, a soldier in a Jeep pulled up to ask what we're doing. So we gave the corporal the spiel about the cylinder-head temperature gauge playing up and the water temperature being on the red line.

I still didn't seem to be impressing him. He mentioned that we had landed in the midst of a major Marine Corps exercise and a couple of Hercules transports are due in any minute to airlift them out.

I then gave the spiel about a precautionary landing. He likes the precautionary word.

"You did the right thing, guys," he said. "Anyone else speaks to you, say Corporal Webb said it was OK. Have a safe day."

We worked another few minutes on our pretend fix and then climbed back in. "Where are we off to?" Gerry asked. "I don't know, but let's get out of here before the Hercs arrive," I replied.

Rather than taxi to the end of the runway, we went across to the far side and tried a diagonal takeoff. It was straight into the wind, but gave us much less runway and we were fully laden and the air was getting hot. We did not really think about this in the rush to get away until we just got off the ground and then hit some sink with first one wing, then the whole aircraft, being sucked back down to the ground as the trees approached.

Of course it was the left wing that dropped and the clear space of the runway was to our right. Power was on full and there was no clear ground ahead available to get down on. The choice was power off and into the bottom of the trees or full power and into the tops of the trees, or clear if we were lucky.

It was close. If only we had had a video. I was sure we were goners, it was the closest I have ever been. We climbed to 2,500ft and flew towards the coast without a word being said.

"Right, what are we going to do," I asked.

"Look, just get low and fly along the beach, stuff the marines, what are they going to do," Gerry said.

"Listen, there are three options I see. One is fly back to Southport, which I don't want to do because we have a strong headwind all the way and we will just have to come back this way again when the wind will probably not be so good.

"Two, we can fly back to Topsail Beach and land there, we will be right into wind where the beach goes around the corner and there looked as though there would be some bars and restaurants which we could telephone Cherry Point from, or three, we could land at this TopSail Island/Holly Ridge strip that is meant to be near here but is completely crosswind, probably over the 10mph max for an alpha.

"But flying through the zone is not an option."

"Let's just fly along the beach," Gerry said.

"No."

"Why not?"

"It's against the regs, they'll pull my licence, they've got guns, they've got jets that do 500mph, they've got radar, we cannot escape them."

"Let's just go along the beach, they'll never spot us."

"Look, how many microlights like this are there around. And we've got a Golf number on the wings. No way."

All the time this went on we were flying in a circle over the coast, not knowing whether to head north, west or back south.

Finally, I decided on the Holly Ridge airstrip. I could not face going back to Southport and did not know how hard the sand on the beach was, so a maximum crosswind landing on a regular airstrip seems the only answer. Oh well ...

Gerry was not too happy, he moaned in the back that I'm chicken. I told him to shut up. The atmosphere got tense, I think we were both a bit stunned from the narrow escape on that last take-off.

Holly Ridge is an east-west grass strip in amongst trees. In a cutting along the western end there is a set of power cables at the runway threshold. The descent was bumpy, so I pulled on speed to cut through any thermals. Just as we were 100ft over the wires... WOAHH.

The left wing took a huge dip ... it felt like a 60 or 70 degree roll, although it must have been less. Gerry instinctively grabbed the right flying wires and heaved on them as I struggled with the bar. A moment later we were down; not an elegant landing, but in one piece.

It was not even 11am and we had almost killed ourselves twice in less than an hour. Time for breakfast, I said.

In the restaurant in the nearby town, most of the customers had very short haircuts. This was definitely a military zone. On the way back to the airfield, I stopped at a telephone box to call the Cherry Point control tower.

"Hi there, I'm in an ultralight at Holly Ridge and would like to get through the restricted zone R5306D."

The Marine Corps were not helpful. "We've a major exercise on at the moment, sir. No can do."

I mentioned that we had tried to raise them on the radio and failed, so being responsible pilots we had landed to get clearance. What about R5306 B, C and D? I asked. "Sorry sir, call back on May 20," the marine in the tower said. This is four weeks away.

"Listen, I am trying to fly up to Kitty Hawk and then across the States, I cannot wait that long. Surely you are going to stop the wargames sometime for a cup of java or something. We only need 20 minutes," I pleaded.

"Look, we are marines. We do not stop for coffee," the tower replied. "You have two choices: fly inland and around the zones or go five miles off the coast. That is it."

Well, it was something to think about that afternoon as we lay in the sun. (Gerry only learned to swim last year. Our airfield at East Fortune is on the south of the Firth of Forth, so to go north you need to cross six miles of water ... and who wants to make a forced landing and survive only to realise you do not know how to swim?)

The crosswind still worried me. The Pink Panther climbed like a pig with the two of us on board – Gerry at 195 pounds, me at 210-ish. So with all the trees around I liked to use the full length of any runway available so if the engine died on take-off and we could not land dead ahead we would, hopefully, by then have enough height to turn back.

A potential problem at Holly Ridge was a house in a clearing at the far end. Would the wind whip around the tree-line there and cause problems as we took off? The rotor from the cutting for the power lines on landing was bad enough.

I set out to pace the runway. Halfway down, a pack of dogs raced from the house and pounced on me. I didn't stand a chance against the ten of them. As I swung round to beat one off, two more moved in. My only thought was that if I lost my footing and fell then that would be the end. As I pushed my forearm towards one gaping mouth, another dog snapped at my calves. Then my trousers started to rip ... a bite to my waist and they were torn off me, left hanging from one leg.

As I wondered why Gerry wasn't coming to help – he must have heard my shouts – I began to plan killing the dogs one by one. Even a good stomp on a front leg should break it and put them out of action ... or would they just get even more frenzied?

"What are you doing to my dogs? My babies, my babies," cried this enormous middle-aged woman as she waddled from her house.

"Get them off me. NOW!" I yelled.

"Oh God, oh God, my babies. This has never happened before, I'm sorry, so sorry," she wept between screaming at her dogs and trying to lead them away from me.

At last the pack was back in its pound. The woman's father, who had been mowing grass at the other end of the strip then arrived to help. All I needed was some antiseptic cream, I told them. And a pair of trousers!

The lady insisted the dogs had had all their injections, including rabies, but she would take me to the hospital for a check-up if I wanted.

"A cup of tea and a bandage would do fine," I replied. Not really stoically, it was just that I thought we would never get away from the airfield before dark if I got stuck waiting in a hospital. And I was definitely not spending a night near those dogs, however strong their cage.

As I made polite conversation, I was asked what I did for a living. "Oh I'm a journalist, I write about business and the stockmarket," I replied. "But I originally trained as a lawyer." The woman went white with shock for the second time. I thought she was in a worse state than me.

A few days later, on a wet afternoon in Kitty Hawk, I realised why. Every advert on daytime television was from lawyers inviting people to sue for personal injuries. One of them had a memorable telephone number: 1-800-GET-CASH. I wonder how much four dog bites – one still visible when I left the US at the end of my trip – were worth?

I realised the woman must have been worried that I would sue or, as I discovered later, have her dogs impounded because of the rabies problem. So I tried to point out that I was a fully-grown ugly sort of person, who would recover. But it could easily have been the kids of a family stopping off at the airfield, or what would have happened if the dogs had run out as an aircraft was taking off?

Yes, the old traditions of physically pacing out a strange runway have their benefits after all. A couple of bites was better than a crash.

To allay Gerry's fears, I gave him the only lifejacket and we discussed a sea ditching procedure. We had heard that a group of pilots flying across the English channel had been told that the British Microlight Aircraft Association recommended method was to climb out at around 300ft and hold onto the rear undercarriage until just a few feet above the water. This did not sound very practical. Neither did sitting in the machine until it hit the water at around 25mph, if one got the stall just right, and then try and fight clear of the rigging under water while recovering from the deceleration.

I decided, as pilot, that Gerry would jump at around 20ft while I tried to keep control and then I would put the machine in a turn and follow him. That settled, off we went, waypoints three miles offshore punched into the GPS.

With the strong southerly, we headed out to sea bearing due east. The GPS said the first corner of the zone was 10 miles away.

"Turn back, turn back, I'm not flying 10 miles out to sea," Gerry urged.

"Shut up, we are not going 10 miles offshore. We are going three miles, exactly three miles, and we will be at 5 or 6,000ft, so will be able to glide back to the beach, stop panicking!"

"Look, the GPS says we have ten miles to go and we are heading straight out to sea. You must have programmed it wrong again. Turn back, I am not going that far out to sea, I don't care if we have to go the long way round inland. This is NOT fun!"

In his panic, Gerry could not appreciate the difference between track and heading. There was nothing for it. "Look, I am the pilot. I am flying us EXACTLY three miles off the coast and we are not going back. That's it."

The next 20 minutes were some of the longest in my life. All the time I kept having to stop us drifting a little closer to the beach which was clearly visible, if what seemed like a long distance away. It was that old thing, if you look at something too hard, you will fly towards it.

Of course we never saw a single aircraft between us and the beach. We could just have flown along at 200ft and no-one would have known. Once we made that turn back to land, I started breathing again. Ten minutes later we were on finals for Michael Smith field at Beaufort, NC.

It had taken an hour and 15 minutes to fly the 53 miles (as the crow flies) but it was the longest flight I made in the whole trip.

If you every get the chance to fly into Beaufort, grab it. A lovely town and a great little FBO with a white porch where you can while away an afternoon watching the arrivals and departures, chatting with other pilots.

Accommodation is pricey, although Michael Meadows, the Chief Flying Instructor, does a great job trying to fix you up with a good deal ... even pretending that someone else who is really fully-booked was offering a cheaper rate!

That night we treated ourselves to a few well-deserved beers and chatted to a few locals.

The following day was the start of a weekend music festival and the forecast was for thunderstorms – it looked like we had found a good place to rest up. The problem was, all the accommodation was booked up. Our saviour was a fisherman called Pete who had offered to let us spend the night on his boat, Miss Nonie. It was an easy one to remember, it had the same name as one of the reporters who was the bane of my life back in Edinburgh.

In the afternoon, after trying to explain to the hotel keeper that the pilots he was expecting that day would not be arriving because of the same weather that was keeping us there, we met up with Pete on Front Street after spending the day watching the yachts come and go ... or, as in the case of the America, a beautiful $15 million reconstruction of an antique boat, come and stick, right on a sandbar at the harbour entrance.

It was five dollars to go aboard and have a look around, but there were few takers. We had all had enough entertainment free of charge!

By now the weather was too bad for the 2nd Marine Aircraft band, so they cancelled their open air concert. Gerry had been looking forward to seeing his tormentors at close quarters, so to ease his disappointment we went for a beer.

Pete's favourite chat-up line with the girls was: "Want to have a ride on my Trojan?" He, of course, meant his Trojan 34 boat – and not the well-known brand of condom. At least he said he did.

My most successful line was turning my back on a lady. Pete, Gerry and myself were chatting to her at the bar when she realised her blouse was becoming unbuttoned, so I turned away and gave her something to hide behind while she sorted things out. As happens everywhere in the States, we discovered a couple of pilots in the bar and while Gerry and Pete talked to them I got to know Susan Murray, a surgical assistant, a little better.

Later, leaving the live music in the Back Street Bar to see if the salsa band was going to brave the elements, I got a gentle knockback when I tried to put an arm around her. Gerry was luckier. Two guys he was talking to in the pub asked him if he'd like a blow job!

The first I knew was when he came over to Susan and I and said: "....for f***'s sake, those two guys just asked me if I wanted my c*** sucked". They'd asked the wrong guy, I have rarely seen two people leave a bar so quick. If they had asked any of the fisherman there I think they would have left through the windows. Ditto if Gerry had not been so stunned, I'm sure. From now on, though, when Gerry got on my nerves I would start calling him Pretty Boy.

I had offered to give Susan a flight in the Pink Panther and said I would call her at her hotel in the morning. Well, after a short sleep on Miss Nonie, Gerry and I were up not long after dawn and in a taxi to the airfield.

I did not really think it was fair to wake Susan up ... and then, over the taxi radio, I heard her voice ordering a cab back into Beaufort so she could pick up her truck. She was really surprised to hear me on the radio saying we were on the way to the airfield, but half an hour later she was strapped in and, Clear Prop!, we were off for a 10-minute trip around the harbour. As Pete would no doubt have said, it is one way to get between a woman's legs.

The air was a smooth as could be, but a couple of tiny bumps made Susan grip a little tighter. Someone sitting so close cannot hide their nerves. On finals, just a few moments before touching down, I saw the shadow of the aircraft on the grass to our right. Thinking it was a pretty sight, I told her to look down.

"Is that something we have to watch as you land?" she asked. "No, just thought it was something nice," I replied casually, before making a really good landing where we just floated on and on before touching down.

Phew! At least I have given a good impression of microlighting, I thought. If only she had known she was my fourth ever passenger.

Susan said she had taken a few flying lessons in the past, and was tempted to take it up again. A few months later, when I spoke to her before returning to the States for a wedding, I realised she had been even more nervous than I had thought ... although she had enjoyed the experience.

As we said goodbye, she I mentioned she was heading up the Outer Banks, so I told her we might be stopping over at Ocracoke or Cape Hatteras that night. If she was heading that way and wanted to meet up, it might be worth going down to the airfields there.

As it was, we made reasonable time to Ocracoke, where there was just a runway and no facilities, and thought we would just press on to Billy Mitchell field, half an hour away at Cape Hatteras. We had also had an "interesting" cross-wind landing at Ocracoke, so that was another reason for pressing on. Once round the cape we'd have a tailwind. It was a beautiful flight, the air smooth and the beaches deserted. But under the left-over clouds from the previous day's storm the Atlantic was a cold and steely grey.

Billy Mitchell field had a runway, apron and large shelter with a telephone box and phone book and an automated weather station. Underlined in the telephone directory was the local cab company, so we decided to stop for lunch and fuel up from the local gas station.

A reticent driver told us the nearest restaurant was Bubba's rib house, so it was beef for breakfast – no mad cow disease here. On the way down the road, the cabbie nearly swiped a motorcyclist off the road. The angry biker looked as though he wanted to hit somebody ... we took his side when told the bill was $10 for a five-minute ride.

"Do you have a brother who works at Hilton Head?" Gerry asked. I explained that we thought he was expensive. "I'm the only taxi here, and it was a ten-minute drive just to pick you up," he told us. We walked back to the airfield.

Soaking up the sun in the sand dunes, it was hard to image that just out to sea across the regimented lines of rolling waves was where the key display of the true military potential of aircraft had been carried out.

Billy Mitchell enlisted as a private in the US Army at the outbreak of the Spanish-American war of 1898. An excellent military record led over 18 years in the Signal Corps led to a staff posting in Washington where he paid for flying lessons at a civilian school and then persuaded his superiors to send him to the Western Front to study Allied air tactics. He saw there that a nation's airforce should be an independent service, that control of the skies was a critical part of a successful advance, and that air power could cripple an enemies lines of supply and communication. On 1 September, 1918, he proved his tactics when he sent a force of 1,476 aircraft in support of the US advance at St Mihiel.

A few weeks later, Mitchell proposed that the army form a parachute division, but no-one would take his idea seriously. In his crusade for an independent airforce, Mitchell claimed in front of several Senate committees that aircraft had made the navy's battleships obsolete. His chance came in 1921 when it was announced that several German warships taken as prizes under the Treaty of Versailles were to be destroyed in naval ordnance tests. On 21 July, a squadron of 11 of his bombers sent the Ostfriesland to the bottom just off Cape Hatteras with two direct hits and four near misses.

"In the development of air power, one has to look ahead and not backward and figure out what is going to happen, not too much what has happened," reads the quote from Brigadier General William "Billy" Mitchell, USAS, inscribed on a on a memorial plaque at the airfield. Tragically, a Sunday morning in Hawaii 30 years later showed that it was the Japanese rather than the Americans who had taken his advice.

A telephone call to John Harris at Kitty Hawk let him know we were within hailing distance and planned a 6:30pm arrival. Just before 5:30 we were in the air for the 60-odd mile flight to where it all began, 94 years earlier.

Well, the first five miles to Cape Hatteras itself were rough; windshear around the point, I suppose. I stayed at 2,000ft but it was still tough going for a while. Wonder how Susan would have felt!

What was bizarre to our Scottish eyes were all the people who had driven their cars almost right into the surf at the point, what is wrong with flying there? No, to be serious, I cannot understand why people who have taken the effort to reach a serenely-beautiful and remote place like this do not leave the car behind and walk down and sit by the ocean looking out to Africa with nothing but the sound of the sea and the sight of the surf and sand around them.

Further up the coast, we were down to 500ft. The whole area is a nature reserve and the sectionals request a minimum altitude of 2,000ft, but I did not think we were going to scare any wildlife. The sight of such a strange bird would probably have brightened up their evening.

Well, we were going to be late. The morning's tailwind had vanished, so it was just after 7pm when we joined the circuit at Dare County. I just could not resist a quick detour on the way in to fly by the Wright Monument. At last, a week after leaving Lakeland, we were in that righteous air. It was mind-stretching to think how far flight has progressed in that lifetime since Orville made a 140ft hop at Kill Devil Hills.

Here we were, carrying a fragment of the wing in an aircraft that had been flown across the Atlantic inside another aircraft. Above us, circling in space, were crews of astronauts and cosmonauts. And waiting for us was John Harris, of Kitty Hawk Kites, a man who has probably taught more people to fly at his hang-gliding school than any other person in the world.

A straightforward landing and a taxi over to the terminal and there was John and the airport manager, Tim Gaylord, to greet us. A welcoming party ... we felt like heroes. With the Pink Panther safely hangared for the night – we had to take the wing off, the kingpost made it a few inches too tall to fit the T-hangar – it was off to John's girlfriend's for dinner and a well-needed shower and shave. After all, we had spent the previous night on a fishing boat.

5

Moment Of Truth

*"With a short dash down the runway, the
machine lifted into the air and was flying.
It was uncertain, wavy, creeping sort of flight
at best; but it was a real flight at last
and not a glide."*

Orville Wright, after first flight

Jockey's Ridge is the highest dune in the
United States, its soft sand making it ideal
for teaching people to hang glide. So John
arranged a lesson for Gerry and I to
experience petroleum-free flight at first hand.

My first hang-gliding experience had been
almost 20 years earlier in south Wales. One of my
fellow pupils, Judy Leden, quit college and went on
to become a world champion; I went to university
and took up hot-air ballooning. My abiding
memory was short flights followed by long
struggles carrying the hang glider back up the hill
for another attempt. At John's school, he gets the
instructors to carry your wing back up the ridge.
It's said to be a lot easier than it looks, because with

a little skill you can "fly" the wing up the hill by holding the rigging wires, but I found trudging through the sliding sand hard enough.

After a few short jumps, I managed a flight of 20 or 30 seconds. Although the principles of flight are the same as on a trike, the control movements are quite different in range and feel. The most pronounced was in the landing flare; our poor instructors had great difficulty in persuading us to push the bar right out in the sort of firm and decisive movement that would have caused a massive balloon and stall in the Pink Panther. The smaller wing and lighter load also made the roll control much sharper, it was a question of many rapid and exaggerated movements.

From the moment I clipped in and rested the wing on my shoulders, I felt taken back in time. Not just to the slag-covered slopes of Wales in the 1970s but to those pioneering days when Wilbur and Orville were experimenting with their gliders. It seems obvious now that there is no point in building an aircraft if you do not know how to fly it, but until the Wright brothers, putative fliers seemed to think that their biggest hurdle was just to get into the air; once up, they would work out some way of controlling their aircraft and bringing it and themselves safely back to the ground.

By starting off my trans-continental voyage with a Rogallo wing glide at Jockey's Ridge, I felt I was in a small way paying homage to the breadth of the Wrights' wisdom.

Sheltering from the rain the next day on the lee side of the Wright Monument, I read the letter from Lester D Gardner which was sent with my Kitty Hawk relic.

"The Flyer's efficiency resulted from the Wright Brothers' experiments with gliders. It was first tried on December 14, 1903 on the wind swept sand dunes of Kitty Hawk on the ocean shore of North Carolina about seventy miles south of Norfolk, Va. A toss of the coin decided who was to make the first flight.

"Wilbur won and took off the track and was in the air three-and-a-half seconds, covering 105ft. But the machine swung around, dug its skids into the sand, broke one of them. Several other parts were broken, but the damage was not serious. Thus, Wilbur was deprived of the honor of making the first successful controlled powered flight in history.

"About 10:30am on December 17, after the machine had been repaired, it was Orville's turn. There was a 27 mile wind. Wilbur ran alongside the right wing until it lifted from the 60ft track. Its 'altitude' then was two feet!! The flight lasted only 12 seconds but it made history. The distance covered was about 120ft from the point at which it rose into the air. The speed was 45ft per second and the length of the flight was equivalent to about 540ft made in calm air.

"It was the first flight in the history of the world in which a machine carrying a man had raised itself by its own power into the air in full flight, had gone forward without reduction of speed, and had finally landed at a point as high as that from which it started."

An out-of-season beach resort in poor weather is not the ideal place to hang around, so with the late evening forecast hinting of an early morning opening in the weather, Gerry and I decided on a dawn start. Despite its beauty, I was anxious to put the Carolina coast behind me and head, at last, for the Pacific. Until now, I had been flying in the wrong direction, heading north-east from Florida.

Gerry had a more prosaic reason for his urgency; his flight home was due to leave Sanford, Florida, in two days' time.

As we climbed into the taxi, the pre-dawn glow and light wind confirmed the good forecast. Unfortunately we hadn't topped up the tanks when we landed because we had arrived so late on the Saturday night, and as we rustled up some fuel at Dare County the wind began to pick up. So after leaving a note for Tim Gaylord, the airport administrator, thanking him for his hospitality we decided to take off while we could and enjoy the tailwind.

Well, Gerry decided we should make the most of the tailwind.

My intention had been to head north across the Roanoke Sound to the Wright Monument and do an early morning touch and go next to the launch rail before swinging around to the east.

"No way," Gerry replied. "With that wind we'll be out over the water for hours."

"Nonsense, it's only about five miles. Won't take us more than 15 minutes or so. Look, here it is on the chart."

"But what about the crossing back to the mainland," Gerry replied. "No way, I am not going out over the water again. I don't care who wears the life jacket.

"Promise you are going to go straight to the mainland or I am going to find some other way of getting back to Florida even if I have to walk."

So as we made a long circuit around the airfield to build up height to cross the Croatan Sound I turned my back on Kitty Hawk, promising to return. After dropping Gerry off in Raleigh, I would be on my own. For better or worse, from now on the decisions would be mine alone.

Route 64 was our landmark, and possible refuge. Apart from being in the middle of a corridor between bombing ranges on the land to the south and in Albemarle Sound to the north, it also gave us a good chance of survival, we decided, in case of a forced landing in the Alligator River National Wildlife Reserve. In the event of an emergency, who would the rangers protect? Gerry took no chances; while I kept a look out for other aircraft, he scoured the ground for reptiles.

Of course, weather being what it is, as soon as we were above 1,000ft, the tailwind disappeared so it took us 50 minutes to cover the 50 miles to Edenton. The long bridge over the sound pointed straight into the circuit and eased Gerry's concern about a descent over water.

The runway layout, a wartime pattern made complex with various sections marked off with crosses as unusable, was a reminder of our home base at East Fortune, near Edinburgh, where despite acres of Tarmac we have just a few hundred yards of concrete available. Here, the runway lengths were slightly more generous and we found ourselves refuelling next to a Cessna Citation.

One question asked by many people on the trip was why refuel so often when I could carry 12 US gallons, about 45 litres, in my two tanks, giving me a total endurance of around five hours. The simple reason is that because of the possibility of airlocks I do not like to rely on switching tanks in mid-air. Another is that unless you are trying to set a speed record, why not stop after an hour or two and stretch the legs, look around and have a chat. As someone said, I'd rather have a two-hour bladder and a three-hour tank than the other way round.

But the main reason is that I don't have a panel mounted fuel gauge, relying on the Mark I eyeball instead. Although the tanks are opaque, the belly one is tucked under the back seat and hidden under the cloth apron around the cockpit. A small plastic window in the apron lets you see if the tank is around half full because then you can see the petrol swilling about, but otherwise it is impossible to tell if it is almost full or almost empty. The dye in the oil makes little or no difference once the tank has a few years worth of dirt ingrained on its surface.

The main tank is under the engine and is marked on the side in two-litre increments, so you can keep an eye on the fuel level. My usual way of flying is to use the main tank and fill it up whenever possible, keeping the belly tank as a reserve in case I turn up at an airfield with no fuel available.

Anyway, we picked up a Coke and a couple of gallons of 100ll and decided to head for Tarboro-Edgecombe, marked on the chart about half-way to Raleigh and with a single, almost east-west runway. Good place for an into wind landing and a chance to grab some lunch and wait out the midday thermals, I thought.

For me, flying over all the trees that cover North Carolina was more worrying than over-water trips. There are those that have had engine failures, and those that haven't had engine failures ... yet. My engine quit on me when I was still doing supervised solo flights before sitting my general flying test. Fortunately it was at 200ft just after take-off, so it was just a matter of following the rehearsed engine failure in the circuit routine.

With a 100 hours of flying time ahead of me, I fully expected another chance to practice my gliding, so I scanned every break in the forest for signs of power cables and tried to guesstimate the width of the roads to see if my wing would clear the trees at the edge.

Tarboro was little more than a crop-dusters' strip, so after a look around the small hangar and the storage tanks and pumps we lay in the sun for half an hour before deciding to battle the thermals and find lunch.

Half an hour later we were 26 miles down the road at Wilson Industrial (W03). We liked the idea of its three runways and the fact that unlike its neighbour Rocky Mount Wilson (RWI) there was no regulated airspace. An airfield identifier that is all letters and no numbers also suggests commercial passenger flights, another reason for 50mph fliers to keep away.

With 131 miles, but no breakfast, under our belts we were deserving recipients of a courtesy car to head into town for lunch. A quick telephone call to Todd in Raleigh sorted out the arrangements for the evening and we agreed an ETA of 7pm at Triple W, a field south of the city.

Todd had reminded us that the rigging on the 2,000ft television towers near his home at Clayton did not cross the main highway, so as long as we kept the road between us and the masts we were safe. The tops were 2,328ft above sea level, so as an extra precaution I made sure we were at 2,800ft as we flew by.

Despite this, the masts seemed to have an almost magnetic attraction, drawing us into their lethal web. They had already claimed two lives: one mast was a replacement for two towers brought down when an aircraft flew into the wires.

That danger past, all we had to do was find Triple W, a notoriously well-camouflaged strip hidden among trees. GPS to the rescue once again. About two miles out I spotted a hangar and noticed another aircraft about 1,000ft below us. "Triple W, this is Golf Mike Whisky X-Ray Uniform, two miles east at 2,500ft requesting advisory and information on aircraft about 1,000ft below."

"Hey there Colin," came the reply. "Well spotted. The other aircraft is out looking for you to lead you in. What are you doing way up there? Everyone thought you'd be tree-hopping."

As Todd's friends helped us derig and refuel the Pink Panther, we faced the usual barrage of questions about how a trike flies. Again, I tried to persuade Todd to come for a ride. But despite our success in making it from Florida in one piece he was still unimpressed by the apparent flimsiness of it.

"Years ago, I'd have flown with anyone in anything," he explained. "Now I've got thousands of hours logged and a wife and children, I'm more cautious. I just couldn't tell whether that thing was safe or not."

Back in Scotland nine months later, I had cause to remember that remark. I had arranged to drive from Turnhouse Flying Club in Edinburgh to look at an RAF Hunter that was for sale in Perth, 40 miles north. An older man heard me talking to my friend John Millar who was coming up too and said he was flying to Perth, did we want to come along for the ride. I was all for it, but John mumbled something about there being a few other things we had to do as well.

In the car I asked John why he'd turned down the flight. "Didn't you recognise him? That's the man who landed on the roof of a Mercedes stopped on the public road at the end of the runway at Insch and then blamed the woman driver for parking there." An hour later we arrived at Perth to find the air-sea rescue helicopter was out searching for his missing plane. Tragically, both he and his new wife perished when it flew into a mountain descending from cloud a few miles further north.

Back at Todd's home, Gerry and I said our goodbyes. Next day he was off to Florida on a scheduled flight, just a few hours to undo a week's adventure.

As I fell asleep, I calculated that our flight time for the day of 3 hours 35 minutes for the 175 miles from Kitty Hawk gave a groundspeed of almost 50mph. My dreams were filled with visions of skimming over the Pacific surf within a few weeks.

Little did I realise that it would take me almost a fortnight just to get out of North Carolina.

With Gerry in the back and two full tanks we had probably been well over the weight limits. I had two options if I was to get the Pink Panther light enough to cope with desert heat and high altitudes: a crash diet to shed a few dozen pounds, or some ruthless pruning of my luggage.

I tore the essential pages out of books, rationed myself to a single change of clothes, and re-examined my equipment. Since I couldn't see a lifejacket being much use in Texas, I added it to the pile of bits and pieces for Gerry to take home.

By the time Todd was finished work and we got out to Triple W it was already getting late. My plan was to make a short hop to Fran's Front Porch, a renowned restaurant next to a runway and get a good dinner before heading off early.

I knew where I wanted to put everything, but I had never strapped it all in before. Some things, like my camping stove, I had only bought the day before I left. Todd could not believe I had not had a dry run back home. I tried to explain that I had been so busy working and acquiring all the bits and pieces that there just had not been time. Anyway, I knew where I wanted it all to go because everyone at East Fortune packs the same way when heading off on trips to the islands off Scotland's west coast.

The sleeping bag was stuffed in the nose; a small backpack, a straw hat and my Macintosh laptop computer went under the seat; the tent sat on the back seat with the rucksack strapped on top of it and a small bag for light things like tee-shirts hung over the engine cover.

On the floor of the cockpit I had a two-gallon bottle of water and tucked in various corners were bottles of two-stroke oil. The two map pockets held spare batteries, film and a camera, while maps were in a board strapped across my legs.

I was ready to go, but Todd insisted I did a test flight with everything loaded. An evening gloom was now beginning to settle around the airfield, so I reluctantly agreed to make a short flight and postpone my departure until the morning.

After dinner, when the children had gone to bed, Todd sat up on the sofa and said: "Look Colin, why not forget about all this. If you want to fly to California, stay here a few days, I'll take a fortnight off and we'll take the Cessna and have ourselves a few good times.

"There's no point in killing yourself. I saw how nervous you looked tonight. There's no record to be set here; you'll not be the fattest, shortest, tallest pilot to do it. So why bother? If you want to have a good time away from the office, that's fine. Let's go to Vegas."

Now was the moment of truth.

6

Head For The Hills

*"If you don't get in that plane you'll regret it.
Maybe not today, maybe not tomorrow, but
soon, and for the rest of your life."*

Humphrey Bogart in *Casablanca*

Not being a gambling man, I turned down Todd's offer of a trip to Las Vegas and gave the Pink Panther an extra careful checkover before I departed the following morning. I definitely didn't want to be embarrassed by bits falling off!

In the shelter of the trees, the wind was light, but headwinds were forecast aloft. Watching an aircraft ahead of me, I saw its wings waggle as it broke into the clear air so decided to build up speed after take-off and hug the ground for a while before punching though into the open air.

Todd later told me he thought I was having problems climbing out above the trees because a last-minute present of a gallon of two-stroke oil from one of his friends had overloaded my machine.

My destination was Rowan County, home strip of Jack Neubacher, a columnist on Todd's newspaper, the *Southern Aviator*. But with a 30mph headwind at 1,000ft I knew I was going to have to stop somewhere for a break.

Heading for Siler City made double checking my drift against the GPS straightforward. Halfway there, and visible from Triple W, were the chimneys of a power station providing a perfect landmark. The only problem was they seemed to be moving towards me very slowly! A check on my GPS showed a groundspeed of just 21mph.

A diversion to the north around Lake Jordan to try and fly with one of the dozen or so pairs of bald eagles that winter there was tempting until I checked my fuel. Rather than change tanks in mid-air, I kept on track.

After refueling and grabbing some lunch in Siler City, I spent the afternoon sunbathing and chatting about Scotland with Nancy Moses at the FBO's office. The influence on the South of those God-fearing Scottish pioneers is everywhere. The local liquor laws being one obvious example. Not only are there strict limits in North Carolina on the strength of beer, you are also not allowed to carry more than two bottles of spirits in your car. It must make organising a good party interesting.

Nancy's dream was to come to Scotland, she said, so I promised to send some postcards. Like most people I got chatting to, she asked the three big questions: Is there a Loch Ness Monster, have you seen *Braveheart* and have you got a kilt? And the Scottish tourist board wants to banish tartan from all its advertising.

The winds were forecast to drop towards evening, so when I took off just after six I thought the 57 miles to Rowan County would not take much more than an hour. Nearly two hours later it was sunset and I still had about four miles to go. The main tank was down to its last half gallon of fuel, but at least with a clear plastic tank you know that what you see is what you get. In the last of the light I joined the circuit and taxied up to park alongside Jack's Piper Tri-pacer.

"Hey, thought you'd got lost or something," he said. "You only just made it before dark. And it looks as though you only just made it with the fuel. Boy, that was cutting it fine." His worries eased when I explained about the long-range tank. "Don't like changing tanks unless I'm over a big flat area too," he said.

Back in Florida, Jack's story about me in *Sun'n Fun Today* said the show brings out a bit of adventurism in all of us, but some carry this adventuresome spirit further than others. "Aye, and why not go for a wee bit of a flight all the way 'cross America?" he quoted me as saying. I think he must have a interesting past; he knows the three essentials of a great adventure: good food, a good bed and a hot shower.

After a meal with the family, it was another comfortable night's sleep. I was beginning to wonder why I bothered bringing a tent and a sleeping bag. Jack has a factory in England as well as the business in North Carolina. But he still finds time to restore his Tri-pacer, write a magazine column and fly. Living proof of the old adage: if you want something done, ask a busy man.

In the morning he was down at the factory before the shift started to keep an eye on things and then he dropped me off at the airfield. As the dawn vanished the wind picked up, and at 1,500ft the headwind slowed my groundspeed down to 14mph. A dull, frustrating and increasingly bumpy hour and a half later I was at Statesville.

The forecast was poor, Flight Service promised moderate westerlies for 48 hours, and I began to wonder if I had got it all wrong heading into the wind. Coming the other way, I would have been covering the ground at 80mph instead of 20mph. At 11am I wrote off the rest of the day and got a taxi into town to find a motel.

Mary Jane Parsons at the FBO office told me to look on the bright side: I'd landed in the middle of a party weekend. Iredell County is the world's leading producer of breeder chicks, an information sheet in the motel proudly boasted, so it was no surprise that fried chicken featured strongly on the street stalls.

Perhaps it was the Victorian architecture of the town's numerous historic buildings, perhaps it was the ghosts of its Scottish-Irish Presbyterian founders, or perhaps it was just that this was my first night without the company of friends that had me feeling blue. Maybe it was just the weekend forecast and the thought of that morning's 14mph groundspeed ... and 2,000 miles ahead of me.

Whatever the reason, I decided Todd had been right in one thing: a good time and a successful transcontinental microlight flight might not always go hand in hand.

Early on Monday morning, visibility down at the airfield was just a couple of miles. Flight Service said conditions all around were IFR (instrument flight rules, meaning you can't see out the window and rely on cockpit instruments), with pockets of marginal VFR (visual flight rules, meaning if you look out the window you can see where you are going) in between the thunderstorms. On the ground there were no signs of thunderstorms, just heavy clouds to the north with what looked like a few breaks towards the west.

Flight Service had suggested waiting for an hour or two until pilot reports had come in but I was rigged and raring to go, so decided to fly my own weather mission, climbing to a couple of thousand feet and seeing for myself what was out there.

It did not look good. There was nothing to do but sit and wait for a break in the gloom and look around a selection of Douglas DC-3s parked on the ramp. If you ever been in Brussels, you'll know the pub game where you challenge someone to name 10 famous Belgians – there's a web site for cheats! Perhaps the same game could be applied to the DC-3. Almost 11,000 were built, and names I know include C-47, C-49, C-53, Gooney Bird, Spooky, Skytrain, R4D and Dakota.

As I chatted to Mary Jane, a Citation was being refuelled. Its pilot told me it was owned by an Iranian who had furniture factories in Statesville and a house at Hilton Head. He flew him down to the coast twice a week and spent the rest of the time running his own business. I thought the life of a corporate pilot would suit me right down to the ground until I saw the proud multi-engine rated aviator switch instantly into grovel mode as a large Mercedes pulled up.

I got my chance to fly four hours later. A pilot in from Kentucky said the line of thunderstorms to the north was almost stationary so I decided to hop over to Hickory, 25 miles away. The notes on the chart said there was a Flight Service Station at the field, so I would be able to get a better weather update there.

On take-off I only had to climb 1,500ft to see Mt Mitchell ahead. Its 6,870ft peak was dwarfed by the anvil-topped CuNimb thunder clouds to the north. I dropped down to 500ft above ground for the 55 minutes to Hickory as the GPS indicated the wind was not quite as directly on the nose down there. Leaving the Pink Panther rigged – the optimist in me hoped I would hear that the storms were now heading north – I went in search of the FSS.

Hickory used to have a tower until the controllers strike, and now its FSS was being wound down too. The equipment was limited to ancient teleprinters; the agricultural radar at the FBO gave a better weather picture. One advantage was that Greg McGann and his colleagues had some time to chat to visiting pilots. So after a late lunch (very late breakfast) in the terminal's excellent cafe I showed them my GPS, proudly displaying the screen showing I had made perfect 90 degree turns in the circuit.

The FSS windows looked mainly to the south and west, over the runways. All of a sudden, one of the controllers said: "There it comes," and pointed to the north. A black cloud was almost at the threshold of runway one-nine.

As I ran across the apron outside the FBO, two of the guys on the line offered to give me a hand.

Just as we got the Pink Panther into the lee of a hangar the clouds burst. A minute later, she was safe inside, but still bouncing around in the swirling air stirred up by the storm.

After we got ballast tied to the wing, one of the line crew offered me a lift into town at the end of his shift, so I settled down in the pilot's lounge to scour the Weather Channel for signs of a break in the weather.

The ground crew's idea of a pilot is someone who can afford a $50 a night motel room, my ideal is $25 a night – and no cockroaches. So faced with a second night in town, I moved across the road to the Hickory Inn and telephoned Greg at the FSS for advice on how to fill a wet day. "Stay where you are, I'll be down in 10 minutes to pick you up," he said. "And bring your Mac."

I had joked the day before that I had more computing power in my microlight than they had in their antiquated office, what with my laptop computer, satellite navigation system and pre-programmable radio. There were even microchips in my camera. The only problem was that I couldn't get my modem to work.

What I hadn't known was that Greg ran a Web page design company on the side, along with a few other interests I found out about later that day.

With only the occasional IFR flight in and out of Hickory, Greg had plenty of time to consider my telecommunications problem. My US Robotics modem had an American telephone socket, I had Compuserve's local access number for Hickory. and I had bought a US phone cable from the Radio Shack across the road from the motel. I also bought some cable, a plug and some crocodile clips to wire my laptop into the main supply to recharge it. At first, the assistant could not understand what I wanted, then she explained that they were called alligator clips in the States. She also refused to connect up all the components. "You really can't just connect live current to the transformer like that," she insisted. "Lawyers would sue us if anything happened. I'll just pretend I do not know what you are going to do and sell you the parts."

Somehow, although everything slotted into place after all that, nothing worked.

Within minutes, Greg discovered that while the four lines in a UK telephone cable were arranged 1,2,3,4, in a US cable the two middle ones were swapped over to give 1,3,2,4. A pair of scissors and some insulating tape and I was back on line.

I asked where I could buy him a thank-you beer that evening. "Well, I do a Web page for the Old Hickory Brewery, which brews its own beer," he said. "I'll take you there."

A few glasses later, he asked: "Ever been to a table dancing bar? There's one in town I do the Web page for." Of all the liberal arts now flourishing in Scotland, table dancing is not one. So how could I refuse? After all, it was not as though I would be the one making a spectacle of myself.

As it was, I was wrong again. On a quiet Tuesday night, there were almost as many girls as customers in the bar. "Have you ever been in one of these places before?" Greg asked as he bought the beers. "Well don't worry, I'll tell you how it works. First, you'll need some dollar bills."

The club was in three parts; a bar, a section with seats around a catwalk and a lounge area with poles running from floor to ceiling. When first writing this up, I wrote "lunge" area. But that was definitely off the menu. Rule number one, Greg said, was that customers could not touch the girls.

We, of course, sat the side of the catwalk. Every other customer was in the lounge area. Etiquette, as expressed in rule number two, was the reason. If you sit by the catwalk, you get the best view. In return, you have to tip each girl by putting money in her garter. After a four or five minute spot, the dancer moves off to the lounge area and gyrates around the various poles hoping for more tips. A new dancer takes her place on the catwalk.

Of course if you particularly like the way a girl dances, you reward her with a bigger tip and she spends more time in front of you. On a busy Friday or Saturday night, some of the dancers earn $700 to $1,000 each, I heard.

The 20 dollar bills Greg gave me lasted a couple of hours. With each girl doing three routines an hour, I began to get a little more relaxed as Greg chatted away to them and told them who I was – it turned out that one of his other sidelines was being a part-time disc jockey in the club. I didn't ask if he earned anything like $1,000 a night for that!

Then one of the dancers said: "Hey honey, you know you look at me in a strange way?"

"I probably am," I replied. "To tell you the truth, I know where I'm meant to be looking, but it just doesn't feel comfortable."

She must have been happy with the answer, because at the end of the night she came and sat in my lap and "danced". An honour, I was told.

It was long night. A meal at 5am in an all-night diner ended with a fellow customer pulling out a gun and saying: "You guys fly? Take a look at this, it'll pass through any of those airport detectors without being spotted." Almost the whole weapon was made from plastic and carbon fibre. If Jenni the dancer had thought I looked uncomfortable a few hours earlier, she should have seen me then.

I got back to the motel at 6:10, ten minutes after my early morning alarm call. It was a fine clear dawn, but there was no way I could fly. Let's just say I was overtired. To keep the room after 10am I had to pay for an extra night, so the cheaper motel wasn't such a bargain after all.

Before take-off that evening, Greg was out with his camera. If I had known what he was going to do with the pictures, I would have had an extra coffee to perk me up. Anyway, it was after 7pm before I departed, south-west for Rutherford County.

I planned on a short flight there, pitch my tent for the night, leave at dawn for Asheville and then wait for the perfect day to cross the Appalachians. Everyone I spoke to talked about the mountains with awe, and even the chart warned: "Caution: Severe turbulence may be encountered in the vicinity of Mt Mitchell."

From Hickory I had to climb 3,000ft to clear a ridge of hills directly on track. As I got higher, the sun got lower. Over the first set of hills, there was a second, lower ridge a few miles on which hid the Rutherfordton strip. All the time it was getting darker. I decided to push on. My body couldn't take another night out on the town with Greg.

7
Local Hero

"You'll be bothered from time to time by storms, fog, snow. When you are, think of those who went through it before you, and say to yourself: What they could do, I can do."

Antoine de St Exupery, *Wind Sand and Stars*

With the GPS showing three miles and seven minutes to go, I still could not pick out the airfield at Rutherfordton. I tried double clicking on the radio, to activate the runway lighting. For a few seconds, nothing happened. Then, straight across the nose, the full flarepath lit up. I swung onto the downwind leg, flew a short base and turned tightly onto the numbers.

As I taxied up to the hanger, George, James and Russell were closing up the doors. "Where are you headed?" George, the FBO owner, asked. "West," I replied.

James Gresham, an Australian flying instructor at the field, thought this was a great reply, a perfect illustration of what he saw as a cultural difference between planning obsessed Americans and happy-go-lucky Europeans.

Within minutes they had the Pink Panther tucked in the hangar and James offered to put me up in his spare room. He had switched on the runway lights because he was just about to take a student up for a night flying lesson. Once again, my radio seemed unable to transmit.

Russell asked if I was going to the ultralight gathering at Stateline field that weekend. I hadn't even known about it but James said I could stay a few days, so I thought it would be a bit rude to just fly on. I thought that if anyone knows about flying microlights over the mountains, the Stateline ultralighters will.

I took the chance to clean up the Pink Panther, and Russell wired in a new aerial for the radio. James went up for a flight, and Ron McKinney who runs a little burger bar by the gate came up to take some pictures for his gallery of fame. One flight: one lunch. A fair swap.

The next morning, James had a dawn lesson booked in so I decided to fly the Pink Panther stripped of the long-range tank and all my luggage. She leapt off the runway like a homesick angel.

The early morning mist still dusted the hollows as I flew low and fast towards Lake Lure. Like an amphitheatre in the foothills, houses and hotels lined two sides of the lake, leaving nature to play centre stage on the north western bank. I soared up at 1,300ft a minute to take in the whole setting, then pulled on speed and swooped down to skim past the jetties and boathouses. Seconds later I was up and over the trees, throwing the Pink Panther into a 450 degree turn to check all around before diving back down. A bump as I cut through the turbulence of my own wake and then down into the smooth silky air above the water.

This was flying. The Pink Panther, unburdened, was bringing me into her element. My conscious mind was no longer making the decisions, my unconscious had merged with the machine. The faintest whim became reality. We were at one in our enjoyment of the air; no longer man and machine, master and servant.

This was not even a partnership of equals, it was a feeling of wholeness, an overiding sense of purpose and belonging. Do sprinters think of their brain controlling their legs, or do they think of the race? Do migrating salmon worry about the distance they have to swim to breed, or do they surrender themselves to instinct? No longer did I think of how I should fly the machine: do I push or pull the bar this way or that; press harder or softer on the throttle. Now we just revelled in the air.

As I entered my hours in my logbook that afternoon, I realised I had passed the mythical 100 hour milestone in the air over Lake Lure. So it is true after all, gaining your pilot's licence is only the start of learning to fly.

Did Russell realise I was now no longer a fledgling pilot? I don't know, but he came up to me at the end of the day and asked if I could take him for a flight.

"Don't misunderstand me," he said. "But I just want to fly once around the airfield. A nice safe flight with no showing off.

"You see I never fly with other people, but I've flown thousands of hours in all types and never seen anything like that. I'd really like to experience it but I know I couldn't fly it."

Russell watched carefully as I did the pre-flight checks and listened attentively to the pasenger briefing. I told him to climb in. "I'm 200lbs, is that OK," he asked. "No problem," I replied, thinking of the weight of Gerry, the second tank, the computer, bottles of oil etc.

"I wondered if it was important for the weight and balance?" he said. "Ah, well if you look above us you will see that we pivot from a bracket, so with me in front and the engine behind it doesn't make much difference to the balance."

Back on the ground, he gave me the traditional handshake and said he had enjoyed the flight. I'm not so sure he'll be rushing out to buy a trike, though. After I talked us through the take-off and turns onto the downwind leg I asked if he wanted to take the controls for a moment. "No, no, that's not necessary. You just keep concentrating on the flying," he muttered.

After dark, it was my turn to sit in the back as James took a pupil up for a cross-country night flight. We made a couple of touch and goes away from Rutherfordton and I could hear the pupil taking about how different the aircraft felt having the weight of a passenger in the back.

Saturday morning, and time for my goodbyes. Russell gave me a red tee-shirt with a drawing of a Beech Staggerwing and the slogan Free Spirit emblazoned on the front. Just as I was about to go, George quietly reminded me that I still owed eight dollars for fuel. "Oops," I replied, pointing at the tee-shirt. "So it's not that sort of free spirit."

I'd been down near Stateline a day or two before on a flight with a local doctor and seen it from the air, but it still wasn't easy to find second time around. Russell and his son went in a Piper Cub, taking my luggage with them, while James sat in the back of the Pink Panther.

As soon as wee took off, he asked: "Can you point to where Stateline is?" A good instructor never stops. If your GPS battery goes flat and your map blows away, it's good to know a landmark.

Half an hour later, I made the second go-around of my trip.

With a strong 90 degree crosswind on its only runway, Stateline present a few difficulties. At one end, there were open fields until the start of the runway, which was lined by banks of trees. I could see myself getting settled down on finals only to hit a cauldron of troubled air over the threshhold.

An approach the other way offered the dubious attraction of power cables strung across the airfield boundary, but there was the chance of landing in sheltered air between the hangars lining the first few hundred feet of the grass runway.

I was high coming over the wires and still in the air as the first line of hangars ended. The wind whipped into us, the ground downwind sloped into trees, so it was foot down and full power to climb away and think again.

Next time I came in slightly higher, and aimed for the parallel taxiway. A touchdown and turn into wind combined in one and we were rolling across the grass strip dividing taxiway and runway.

"Do you often land on taxiways," James asked.

"Well, trikes don't really like crosswind landings," I explained. "And the brake is not really up to much, so I thought I would use the longer grass to help slow us down. On the other side of the runway the ground slopes quite steeply. Think of the grass as a back-up in case the brake cable snapped."

Once I got the Pink Panther sheltered under the trees, we heard that a trike had flipped over and crashed that morning when it had been caught in the rotor landing in the opposite direction. I think James's appreciation of my flying skills rose a little then. He said he was never worried, it is when a pupil comes in for their third attempt at landing that you really get concerned.

George had called the local newspaper with my story when I arrived at Rutherfordton, so I had asked the reporter BethTatum to give the ultralight weekend a mention if they had space. As it was, my adventure made the front page lead with a four column photograph, pushing to the fringes stories headlined "Woman fined for gesture at Klan rally plans appeal" and "Three families especially thankful this Mother's Day". An unexpected spin-off from the Stateline plug was a member of the public asking me to sign their copy of the article. I had obviously become a local hero. Dancing girls and autograph hunters, this is the life. Fame at last.

I kept on the ground all afternoon, leaving the three-axis Phantom fliers to grab the glory. One of them claimed to have used his ballistic parachute three times because his wings kept folding up in mid air. Looking at his display, I could see why. In Britain, we are prohibited from using emergency parachutes attached to the aircraft, the reasoning being that there is more chance of them going off by accident when that would kill you – say below 200ft – than of you being in a situation where you would need one. Provided, of course, you do not push the machine outside its flight envelope by attempting outrageous aerobatics, especially loop-the-loops.

In the evening, I took up David Morrison, who had moved to Texas but was home for the weekend. It was too bumpy for anything more than a short flight, but at the end he offered me $30. I told him to forget it, if he really wanted to give something then put a few dollars in a beer kitty for the barbecue.

So it was no surprise that I crawled out of my sleeping bag with a heavy head on Sunday. A couple of guys had already flown off only to come back because the headwind was too strong. After a coffee, I thought: "Well, I only want to get to Ashville, that's not even 40 miles away so if I have a 30mph headwind I'll still get there in 2 hours."

I decided to route via Fairview to pick up Insterstate 26 and follow it into Hendersonville, a general aviation field under the panhandle of Ashville Regional's Class C zone. At 2,000ft I was getting a groundspeed of 28mph, what had those guys been worrying about?

WHOA! The bar was almost torn from my hands, my foot slid off the throttle and the machine was flung into a steep left turn. Despite my seatbelt, it felt I was holding onto the bar to stop being thrown out. With a huge heave, I managed to get the wing straight and applied full power to claw back height. In just a few seconds I had lost 500ft, and there was nothing around to indicate where the turbulence had come from.

All around below me were large flat fields, and I weighed up the pros and cons of making an emergency landing. Each time I decided to press on, there was another little shock like the last one and I decided to get down in a big field and camp out. Each time I got the machine settled down again in straight and level flight I decided instead to press on. One thing was off the agenda, a return to Stateline. After the previous day's experiences in the circuit, I was definitely not going to go back and risk another landing with this funny air around.

My GPS gave me the good news that Fairview was just two and a half miles away. It also gave me the bad news that my groundspeed was down to just 4mph, and indicated an estimated time in flight of almost 40 minutes. I could have landed and pushed the machine there faster. A long, very long, half hour later I was at 500ft over the numbers on the threshhold at Fairview. The wind was straight down the concrete and so strong that it felt as though I was flying backwards and about to land on the grass run-off before the runway's start. It was like coming down in a helicopter except for the forward jolt in the instant between my tires getting a grip on the runway and me chopping the throttle.

The landing was the easy part. Taxiing was major problem because when turning crosswind you have to watch for the wind getting under the wing and flipping you over. As I tried to hold the upwind wingtip close to the ground the gusts just slammed it into the earth. Moments later, as I was using both arms to try and lift it, the wind would ease and I would almost over-compensate. Finally I got into the lee of a hangar, pulled the wing off and put up my tent. The airfield was deserted, it was not even 10am and I was already completely exhausted.

A few hours later I was woken by two ultralighters from Stateline who just happened to be driving past on the Interstate and thought they would call in to see who had aircraft parked at Fairview. Their surprise at finding me was all the greater because they were the same two pilots who had turned back earlier because of the headwinds.

The weather forecast for the next few days was "more of the same", so we drove around looking for a cheap motel. It was a fruitless search so we stopped for some groceries and then they dropped me back at Fairview. I also bought a paperback thriller to keep me occupied if I was going to be stuck here for a day or two. As it was, I only got to read the first chapter when Russell flew in from Rutherfordton to check on one of the aircraft.

"Hey, why don't you hop in the back and we'll fix you up with somewhere to stay until the

Jumping with joy: Trying to fly at Kitty Hawk, N. Carolina.
Air freight: With the crated Pink Panther at Sun'n Fun.

Fill her up: Fuel stop in Louisiana, above, with oil well.
Dawn patrol: Misty hollows in the Appalachian foothills.
Beer call: Al, me and Brett, Under-the-Hill in Natchez.

Mystery: Three graves, above, in the New Mexico desert.
Thunderclap: The photographs below were taken three
hours apart from the same spot at Van Horn, Texas.

Desert boneyard: Mothballed jets, above, at CIA airfield.
No place like dome: Biosphere II, below, north of Tucson.

Two miles high: The altimeter, above, goes round the clock.
Prickly heat: A giant cactus, left, at dawn in Gila Bend.
Down Mexico way: The field colours mark the frontier.

Mission accomplished: The Flying Scotsman and the Pink Panther cross the Pacific coast at Oceanside, California.

weather changes." he offered.

It was tempting, but I had been holidaying far too much over the last few weeks. Now I had to be in the right place for the right time to cross the mountains. Thinking through the morning, the wind had been coming straight from Mt Mitchell 40 miles to the north. That must have kicked up a fair bit of turbulence and in the flat North Carolina peidmont it had just kept rolling on until I was swept up in it.

Crossing the Appalachians was definitely going to require just the right day. The only question was how to get away from an empty airfield to wait it out in comfort in Ashville?

The wind usually dies a little before dusk, so I thought I might be able to sneak in the 20 mile flight before nightfall. I struck the tent and packed up the Pink Panther. By 7pm I reckoned it was not going to get any better than this and took off. Ten minutes later I was back down and unpacking again.

However as I came into land this time I had noticed there was an all night filling station at the other end of the airfield. So, with the wing tied down safely and the tent pitched I climbed into the trike, started the engine and taxied down the country road at the back of the runway. It saved me a three-mile hike and I was able to top up with high test gas and take my pick from fried chicken and biscuits and pizza.

By dawn, I was cold and wet. The skies were overcast but my spirits soared when I realised the wind had gone. By 7am I was in the air for Hendersonville. Of course the airport hadn't opened when I arrived so I tracked down the ubiquitous Coke machine for a tinned breakfast and explored. The airport/facility directory listed it as ultralight friendly, but the few machines I spotted in the open hangars looked distinctly uncared for. It turned out the field was up for sale, the most likely buyer a property developer. The owner told me he could no longer compete with just a 3,000ft runway when Ashville had an 8,000ft one and had staff paid for by the county.

The advice for crossing the mountains was to keep west of the Asheville zone and then swing round the north of the city until I picked up the French Broad River which would lead me through to Gatlinburg.

He also recommended filing a flight plan, so if there were any problems someone would first know I had gone missing and second they would know where to look. I openly admitted to never having filed one in my life, so he took me through the procedure and then offered to activate it for me when I took off.

Now all I had to do was fly through the mountains. For my purposes, the weather was ideal. Almost no wind and a grey sky to keep away the thermals and their associated turbulence. The difficult thing about flying in America is trying to grasp the sheer scale of the country. In Scotland, a 50-mile flight from East Fortune would take you east out into the middle of the North Sea, south down beach-covered coast, north-west into the foothills of the Highlands or west across to the islands on the other side of the country. The prevailing wind from the Atlantic is quickly broken up by innumerable folds in the land over a few dozen miles.

Here, the wind travels hundreds, if not thousands, of miles across comparitively featureless ground until it hits the Appalachians. Distance does not seem to sap its energy, rather it appears to build its strength, its resistance to change, making it all the more turbulent when blocked by one of the world's oldest mountain ranges.

Today, a cloud ceiling of around 6,000ft provided perfect shelter for a two-hour crossing. As I flew along the banks of the river, I kept almost level with the peaks on either side of the valley. Where there were no fields available as emeregncy landing sites, the broad road glistened as a refuge when the rays of sunshine pierced the murk to set ablaze its damp surface.

As I was about to begin my descent towards Hot Springs, snowflakes began to clog my visor. The name did not reflect the conditions that day. For a few minutes I began to feel the chill. For warmth and protection in the open cockpit I had only a pair of chinos, a tee-shirt and two sweatshirts under my Goretex flying suit. I just had not expected snow.

Coming out onto the Tenessee plain, the skies cleared and four bright yellow and black biplanes were headed north in formation a mile ahead and a thousand feet below. It was the first time in the States I had seen aircraft flying outside an airfield pattern and I longed to say hello. I was desperate to share the relief of passing my first major hurdle.

More rivers made navigation to Gatlinburg-Pigeon Forge straightforward and for once my radio seemd to work fine. It was obviously my day. I touched down at ten minutes after noon; the two-hour flight was my longest ever.

8

Tennessee Triker

"When once you have tasted flight, you will forever walk the earth with your eyes turned skyward, for there you have been, and there you will always long to return."

Leonardo da Vinci

My first stop in Tennessee and I had stumbled upon the home town of one of the state's most famous daughters – Dolly Parton – and her "homespun fun" theme park, Dollywood. Faced with a $25 entrance fee, I used my press card for the first time in my life to avoid paying.

A blend of ersatz mountain heritage stands shoulder to shoulder with homages to the park's glamorous celebrity shareholder. I think the mix was intended to emphasise Dolly's down-to-earth simplicity, giving visitors a warm glow by making them feel she is just like one of us. Instead, it left me feeling as though I had been covered in a cloying coat of twee.

One section highlighted Appalachian crafts, everything from lye soap to horse-drawn carriages while a museum looks at Dolly herself in mind-numbing detail (although leaving out all the bits the *National Inquirer* or *The Sun* would like to know); and music shows are constantly on the go.

Within an hour, I had had enough and headed along the six-mile strip of motels, fast-food places, clothing factory outlets, themed family attractions and tacky souvenir shops that make up the booze-free town of Pigeon Forge until I reached the small market centre of Sevierville, which with its wooden-floored "old world" general stores and homely cafes serving mountains of Southern food to hungry farmers evoked a less ersatz Great Smoky Mountain ambiance.

There was still no getting away from Dolly, though. A statue of her has pride of place on the lawn outside the courthouse.

Marybelle, the waitress in the restaurant where I had lunch, filled me in on all the details. Dolly Parton was born in 1946, one of twelve children. As a child she lived in various houses around Pigeon Forge, the most isolated of them two miles from the nearest neighbour, and sang every week on local radio, before leaving for Nashville on the day she finished at Sevier County High School.

She scored a major country hit in 1976 with *Jolene*, then adopted a poppier sound and moved into films like *9 to 5* and *The Best Little Whorehouse in Texas*. But what made Marybelle most proud, she said, was that Dolly had refused to tag along with the Nashville stereotype of subservient females and would tackle Christian issues such as rural poverty. I kept quiet that my knowledge of her heroine was limited to the fact that she had an unusually large chest.

The skies were clouding over again but the wind was light and I was itching to get back in the air. I had thought I would have been so glad just to have got over the Appalachians that I would want a night at Gatlinburg, Pigeon Forge's more upmarket "wet" touristic neighbour, to plan the next stage to the Mississippi. But the morning's flight had been so straightforward I just wanted to get more miles under my belt. I had also been warned that a heavy layer of kitsch all but submerges Gatlinburg's genuine Germanic heritage, with the long, narrow main street packed to the point of claustrophobia with gimmicky souvenir shops and wax museums.

Even signs billing the area as the world's greatest centre of discount shops, with more than 200 factory outlets, failed to distract me. After the diversions around North Carolina, however enjoyable, a sense of purpose had returned and I felt driven to get back in the air and on route. Maybe that was a "cup of ambition" I had been drinking from at Dollywood, to quote from one of her hits.

I settled down in the pilot's lounge and examined the charts. There was controlled airspace around Knoxville, but I reckoned the landmarks on the chart would let me cut close to the top edge without infringing it and I decided to aim for Rockwood, 65 miles away. There I could refuel or change tanks and press on for Crossville or Upper Cumberland airports, leaving me around 80 to 100 miles to cover the next day to reach Nashville.

As I flew to Crossville the weather began closing in. The cloudbase fell from 4,000ft to just 1,500ft above ground. And ahead of me the strip at Rockwood was on an escarpment that rose 500ft from the plain. I pressed on. The air was smooth and my Goretex was keeping me dry – although the deteriorating visibility was being made worse by the rain on my visor. And my radio seemed to have packed in again. There was no sound of any traffic on the Rockwood frequency and no-one was replying to my requests for an airfield advisory.

Touching down on the long strip, I taxied over to the hangar only to find the hangar deserted, the office locked and an "out of order" sign hanging on the public telephone. How was I going to close my flight plan? I rummaged through the hangar looking for a back door into the office, found a telephone and let flight service know I had arrived. With no-one around I got back into the trike and was preparing for take-off when a truck pulled up.

It turned out it was a fellow trike pilot, Mark Taylor, who said he had heard the Pink Panther flying over his house and come down to the airfield to say hello. Until then, he had thought his French Air Creation was the only trike in north Tennessee.

A few months later, I flicked through the latest edition of *Trikes R Us*, a US flexwing magazine, and there was his story. Until then, when he said that he had seen me flying over his house, I thought he lived in one of the few properties scattered around this remote strip.

I had just gotten home from work and flying was the furthest thing from my mind. Besides, it was cold and damp outside and although the air was still, it wasn't a day I would call flyable.

I reached into the Jeep to grab my lighter when I heard a funny noise. I thought to myself: "Huh, that sounds like a Rotax. Naw, can't be. I've lived here for 12 years and I've never seen an ultralight fly over. But the noise grew louder and unmistakable. "Dang it! That's a Rotax!" I looked up again and to the southeast, just behind some trees, I saw a flash of pink directly over my house. I could tell it was no ordinary ultralight. It was a trike!

I had assumed that I owned the only trike within a 90 mile radius. But there it was, another trike. I started jumping up and down like a crazed wannabe; but it wasn't working. The pilot didn't see me. I made a mad dash inside to get my radio. "Where's that dang radio? Where? Where?" I spotted it next to the couch, grabbed it and rushed to get outside. The trike was gone. A full 30 seconds of cursing later, I thought:

"OK, he was heading northeast. Where could he be going? Possibly it would be the Rockwood Airport and that was well over 20 miles away. Where else! Where else could he be going? No, it's gotta be Rockwood."

I threw the radio in the Jeep and spun out of the driveway. As I was making my way to Rockwood I still couldn't see the triker. He was gone. I was urged onward as I thought to myself driving down the road: "If he's not there I would back-track and see if he landed somewhere else." By the time I approached Airport Road almost all hope of catching the mysterious triker had faded. But still I continued. Suddenly, there he was, setting up his final. "All right!"

I was out of the Jeep and at the edge of the runway when he taxied up and shut down. "And here I was thinking I was the only triker around for miles," I spoke to him as I shook his hand, not giving him a chance to speak. "Hello," he replied in a funny accent that I didn't recognise. I thought to myself: "Ya know, I don't believe this feller is from around these parts." And he wasn't. Not even close.

His name was Colin MacKinnon from Scotland. Colin had just flown from Gatlinburg-Pigeon Forge Airport on his way west, which he described as "as far as I can go cross-country". When I asked about flying in this weather, the Scotsman remarked that in Scotland "you fly when you can". To him, the few spots of rain he had flown through were no problem.

He had landed at Rockwood for a 30 minute warm up. Too soon for me, Colin decided it was time to move on. He wanted to get to Crossville Airport before dark. We said our goodbyes and the Flying Scotsman flew west. As I was driving back home, I noticed that I wasn't tired anymore and my mood was definitely on the upswing. I couldn't help but think about Colin and his trip to fly across the USA. Then it dawned on me; tomorrow, while I would be at work, Colin would be flying over Nashville. My face grimaced, the nasty mood came back.

Crossville wasn't much of a hop away, 30 minutes later and I had covered the 22 miles to arrive in the midst of a quiet celebration. The Whitson family had just been granted a new lease.

I got a lift down to the local motel, phoned for a pizza and congratulated myself on a record day's flying: 195 miles in five hours. The average groundspeed of 39mph was more like what I had hoped to achieve.

Crossville is a town with a population of just 7,000, but it is known to fliers around the world. The reason: *Trade-A-Plane*, a 200-plus page classified catalogue of aviation dreams, from restored classic to redundant jets ... and a source of information on a few essentials almost impossible to find anywhere else.

The next morning, I heard how the magazine was started by Cosby Harrison after he crashed his plane back in 1937. Trying to track down spares he wrote off to neighbouring airfields, even offering to trade his wrecked plane for one that could fly.

The correspondence turned into an informal newsletter, sharing information about parts and maintenance. When flyers began asking how to subscribe, Cosby launched *Trade-A-Plane*.

Its hallmark, the distinctive canary yellow paper, came about due to Second World War shortages. Cosby found a large surplus of lightweight yellow stock and bought up all he could.

The business is now in the third generation of the family, with Alan Strachan, Cosby Harrison's grandson, running the production side of the business. He told me the demand for four-colour printing on their canary yellow paper had caused a few headaches, until they pioneered printing on white paper and then filling in with yellow ink. Most readers never noticed the change!

By the time I got down to the airfield, it was getting late in the morning and the air had heated up. The Whitsons had missed seeing me land the night before and, I am sure, wondered if the Pink Panther was some kind of spoof aircraft. In general, I found that most ultralight pilots in the US had heard of trikes, but never seen one. Regular fliers never even knew such things existed. So I got a good crowd to watch my take-off.

The air was rough, it must have looked interesting as I made a low pass over the hangar. I probably confirmed their suspicions about this weird British aerial beastie.

In my search for smooth air, I climbed to 7,000ft. But there were still massive bumps in the sky. After 20 minutes I was tired of struggling. Although the textbooks say leave well alone and let gravity do the work in keeping the trike centred below the wing, the temptation to try and damp out the oscillations is irresistible – and tiring. So I decided it was time for lunch at Upper Cumberland.

When Bud Turner of Aviation Sales there heard about my trip, he invited me to eat with him. When he heard that I worked as a journalist, he asked: "Do you know that we have the most technologically advanced newspaper in the world here in Cookeville?

Once again it was time for a media appearance, but this time I took the chance to do a little interviewing myself.

Mike McCloud – with a surname like that he should be a Flying Scotsman too – was the publisher and executive editor. "Several people in the town thought the daily paper was too one-sided, too liberal," he told me. "So they decided to back a new one to give the other viewpoint."

Starting from scratch, Mike was able to invest in the most high-tech of equipment to save on staff and costs. So the photographers used digital cameras – expensive, at $25,000 each, but then it saves on office space and staff and equipment for a darkroom; the office was almost paper free, with stories appearing in print for the first time when a proof was made of the completed page; and the pages were sent to their printer 100 miles away over the telephone lines.

But the biggest shock for me was discovering that two daily newspapers were competing head to head in a town with a population of just 10,000. In Britain, communities five times that size are lucky to have just a single weekly newspaper.

Reporter Karen Beaty gave me a lift back to the airfield with a photographer to finish her story and later faxed a cutting to my paper, *The Scotsman*. Friends at work said she could not believe she had met someone from such a prestigious title. I should have told her we worked in Dickensian conditions in a Victorian building and I was envious of the simplicity of her high-tech operation.

After a prowl around the hangars, there were a couple of ex-RAF Jet Provosts in one, it was time to load up the Pink Panther and head for Nashville. The forecast was for storms and I was feeling homesick for bright lights, so Music City USA seemed the perfect place to lay over. I was about to say goodbye to Bud and had shouted "Clear prop!" when there was a yelp from across the ramp. Bud's dog had been caught in a Cessna's prop, the tip of a blade ripping open his shoulder.

There was nothing I could do to help, so I started up and taxied out of the way to take-off for Nashville. On the hour-long flight to Lebanon I thought of my instructor Gordon Douglas's dog Scooby-doo who got an ear caught in a prop when greeting his master. He now sits poised at the edge of the concrete waiting for the engine to go quiet before leaping into action. I later heard that Bud's dog made a full recovery too.

At Lebanon, I picked up a couple of gallons of fuel and made a quick turnaround. The controlled airspace around Nashville International was daunting, but at the top end, in a little cut-out, was Cornelia Fort. With parallel grass and concrete strips it looked ideal.

The evening air was beautiful, but it was getting dark. My GPS had the limits of the Nashville zone programmed in and the chart showed 1,000ft pylons with a 2,100ft bottom to the Nashvile outer zone. At 1,500ft on the altimeter and almost no headwind, I calculated I would arrive about five minutes before dusk. To the north I could see clouds building, so I felt the quick turnaround at Lebanon had been worth it.

A few miles out from Cornelia Fort, I still could not see the airfield. The ground below appeared to be swamp, not what I expected on the outskirts of a major city. There was no doubt it was Nashville, the multiple runways of the international airport were lit up and beckoning just a few miles to the south. I began to consider what I would do if I could not find Cornelia Fort. There was not enough light left to return to Lebanon. Could I radio Nashville International? Even if I landed there, how would I find my way around its taxiways?

A moment later, there was the airfield, tucked in a bend of the river, the hangars in the lee of a hill. A straight in approach and I was down. As the last of the light faded I found a space amongst the ranks of parked aircraft and went to ask about fuel and parking.

"You can't stay here," the man on the line said. "Mr Colemill doesn't allow ultralights here. You'll have to go."

"What do you mean. It's dark. I can't go anywhere now," I said.

"Well you should have contacted us before coming here, then you would have known."

"Why should I have contacted you. I checked your entry in the US Government directory of airfield facilities and it doesn't say no ultralights. If he doesn't like ultralights, he should have let them know like other airfields do. Anyway, I can't go anywhere tonight and bad weather is forecast for tomorrow. Is it OK to park where I am or do you want me to move?"

Although the chap was in a golf buggy, he made no offer to run me back over to my machine, so I had to unload and remove the wing myself. As I was parking the trike over the A-frame and tying the noseplates to a stake I had hammered into the ground, the man came back over.

"Hi. I'm Tony. Where have you come from? What's it called? How did you fit all that it? Is that a GPS you have there?" His questions gave me a chance to point out the Golf number and mention that it was a British registered aircraft, that I had a British licence and that the machine was fully insured.

"It's a British aircraft?"

"Yes. That G-MWXU on the wing there, that's our version of an N number."

"Well, I reckon Mr Colemill might make an exception since you are British. But I know he won't want a lot of ultralighters coming in here. You can't go anywhere now it's dark, so I better give you a hand."

In the office was a white-haired gentleman with shoe-lace tie who looked as if he owned the place. He never said a word.

Despite Tony Ricetti's initial stand-offish attitude he even gave me a lift to a cheap downtown motel. A walk across the river and I was in Second Street, where the guidebooks said the action was. Of the dozen or so bars and restaurants, the Market Street Brewery looked the most appealing. A good steak and a couple of beers later I asked for the bill. Twenty minutes later, no-one had come back to get my signed credit card slip. In a rash moment, I decided that if no-one could be bothered to collect my money, I was just going to leave.

For the rest of my stay in Nashville, my guilty conscience made me avoid that bar, and it was the best one that I visited in the city. I need not have bothered, when I got home I found that even without my signature the $15 had been taken off my credit card.

9

Country Culture

Do not believe what your eyes are telling you,
All they show is limitations.
Look with understanding.
Find out what you already know,
And you'll learn the way to fly.

Richard Bach

An article in the newspaper caught my eye. "How about a place where people can go to give in to their creative urges any time they like? Here's hoping the Creative Fitness Center becomes a success. For a nominal fee artistic types can delve into oils, pastels, papier-mache, tie-dye, collage, sculpture and much more. If you are curious, head on over for the grand opening, featuring free food and drink." How could I resist?

The taxi driver warned me it was a strange neighbourhood, but it looked more like a respectable suburb than the seedy commercial area I had expected. It turned out that Whitney Gilbert had converted her house into a multi-media arts centre.

One of her friends said she fancied herself as the "epitome of Nashville artiness". Whitney told me: "I just love the European idea of culture, the way it influences all parts of life. Americans just do not seem to give it the same priority, and that is what I want to change."

Because of some unspoken business connection, most of Whitney's guests had lived in Edinburgh for at least a few months at some stage or another, so for once I was not the centre of attention as an exotic stranger. In fact a Californian who talked about his wine collection and swapped tales of famous vintages with a woman who had lived in Paris and eaten at all the famous restaurants – at $300 dollars a meal – were typical of her friends. This was not the European culture that I know, it seemed like flash, brash Americanism.

A street party the following night with Emmy Lou Harris coming straight from a flight from London to join some friends on stage was more my type of thing. The only hiccup was trying to buy a beer. "Sorry, you need a wristband. You can get one over there," the girl behind the bar said. At a table by the kerb, another girl told me that unless I had something that proved I was over 21 I couldn't get a wristband. "Hey, I'm 35 and bald. Do you think I shaved off my hair just to be able to buy a beer? But thanks for the flattery," I replied. She handed over the essential paper collar.

Maybe it was a legacy of the 19th century temperance crusade. Janey Lee, a lady I met at the street party, told me that in 1877, temperance advocates in the Tennessee general assembly managed to pass a "Four Mile Law" prohibiting the sale of alcohol within that radius of a school. She also told me Tennessee later became known as the "monkey state" after it passed a ban in 1925 on the teaching of evolution in its schools. Despite a high-profile trial of a teacher a year later, the law remained on the statute books until the late 1960s.

I think Janey was glad to see me: she was out for the evening with an old boyfriend and saw me as an ally in case he felt like getting too friendly. It ended up a battle between him and me to see who could out party the other.

The next morning I needed a good strong coffee with breakfast, but at least I was in the right town. Joel Owsley Cheek made Nashville the centre of the US coffee trade at the start of the century. As a grocery salesman he travelled throughout the mid-South by horseback and noticed the growing popularity of the brew. When he became a partner in a grocers, he was the first person to think of blending top quality coffee beans. In 1892 he persuaded the manager of the Maxwell House Hotel to try his latest blend and with the added cachet of the hotel's famous customers behind it, the brand became a worldwide success. I still prefer Nescafe.

That afternoon I telephoned to ask for a lift to the airfield. I wanted to check the Pink Panther over, refuel her and get ready to go when the weather changed. "No problem, sir. We'll be along in 15 minutes." I was wrong, Cornelia Fort was not the most inhospitable airfield I had ever been to.

Two minutes later the telephone rang. "Is that the gentleman with the microlight? I'm sorry, the boss says we are too busy right now to pick you up. Can you just get a taxi?"

Well, it was $20 for a taxi or $25 to hire a car for the day. I decided to see the sights.

The next day the forecast was good and as I readied the Pink Panther for a morning take-off, Tony was on the line again. It took just two gallons to top off the tank. Then Tony said: "Don't worry about paying for that, or the parking fees. It's been good to have you here."

I noticed the back of his hand was a web of fine white scars. "Well sir, I caught my hand in a prop a few years back. There was an old gentleman having problems getting his engine started and he asked me to swing his prop to pull through some fuel.

"Now I tell you, I have done some bad things in the past but I believe the Lord was looking out for me that day. I heard his voice warning me of evil as I approached that aircraft, but I tried to ignore it. That old gentleman had his switches off, but that engine still fired and it caught my hand.

"It took them doctors a long time to fix my hand, but I know I was saved by the Lord. If I had listened to that warning, maybe we would have realised that there was a short in that engine. But He still saved me. How I was not pulled through that propeller, He only knows.

"Let me tell you son, there's God's hand all round these aircraft. My old mother was born the year before the Wright brothers made their first flight. Last year she had to be taken to Raleigh for a major operation and the only way was to fly her there. It was her first time in an aeroplane and the trip saved her life. Is that not an awesome thing?"

Next morning, the old man with the country and western tie was looking every bit the Southern gentleman as he talked to some businessmen in suits. Although I had my tartan flying outfit on again, he still didn't say a word. But Tony's gesture over a few dollars worth of fuel had restored my faith in Southern generosity.

Looking back, I suppose Cornelia Fort is in quite a sheltered spot and the wind was a bit strong. But I never expected the 12 miles across northern Nashville the following morning to take half an hour. A very bumpy half hour.

John C Tune, the relief airport for Nashville, was on my route for Kentucky Lake so I decide to land and spend another day as a tourist. Cornelia Fort is named after the first American woman pilot to die on active duty, a signpost outside the airport said. John C Tune was the inspiration and author of the airport authority charter and the authority's first chairman, a plaque in the FBO reception area explained.

A night camping by the river appealed, so I hired a car for the day and set off to see the home of General Andrew Jackson, the seventh president of the United States and a champion of the "common man" first. Born in South Carolina, Jackson was an orphan by the age of 14. As a lawyer, politician and soldier he excelled. His father died before he was born, his mother and two brothers died in the Revolutionary War. Jackson went on to study law and then led a remarkable victory at the Battle of New Orleans which signified the end of the war of 1812 and the defeat of the British. His home, the Hermitage, has been preserved as it was when the general died. The simple scale of it impressed the most. With just four rooms on each of the two floors, it must have been crowded even before friends and family visited. But it still had an atmosphere of a true home. There were too many trees on the lawns to land a microlight, though.

On my way west to the Kentucky Lake, my next stop was the airfield at Humpreys County. My schoolboy nickname was Humph so I just had to call into the county seat, Waverly. The community couldn't be much bigger than a few thousand homes, but there was a fabulous looking art deco courthouse and a small cinema.

If I'd known how difficult it was to find a campsite by the river, I'd have set up the tent at the airfield and spent the night here. Instead, in the early evening I found a KOA campsite at Buffalo River near I40 to the south. Campsite to Americans means somewhere to hook-up the recreation vehicle, a travelling home from home. But they said they had tent pitches too. It was only after I had paid my money I realised it was in a spot right next to the Interstate. A bush and a thin layer of canvas were all that there was between me and the trucks rolling through the night. At 5am I joined them, heading back to Nashville.

A 7am takeoff saw me retracing my route along the road to Waverly. It was strange how different things looked from the air, the road and railway line in a valley with a low ridge to the north. From the car, all I had been able to see were trees.

An hour and 40 minutes later I landed at Dickson. That early on a Sunday the airfield was deserted, so it was back in the air for the 17 miles to Humphreys County. It too was deserted, not one aircraft on the ramp outside the spanking new terminal building.

An hour's snooze in the sun helped me catch up on my sleep after the early start and then the airfield began to come to life – as a base for radio-controlled aeromodellers.

Just before lunch, while I was talking to the club members and watching their flying, a Piper twin landed looking for fuel. Unfortunately the college student who was looking after the office during the vacation was late for work, and he had the only key for the fuel tanker.

The Piper pilot was not very happy. He had a tight schedule, had telephoned the day before to confirm fuel was available and had not been warned that radio models were being flown at the airfield.

We all did our best to help, eventually finding spare keys in the office. Then we had to find out how the tanker worked. Fortunately the college student arrived and took over.

The pilot was still irritable. "I'm going to write to whoever's in charge of aviation in this county," he said.

"There's no need," one of the aeromodellers said. "You're talking to him."

"Well I'm going to write to the local newspaper telling them about what's happening here," the pilot fumed.

"Don't bother," said Richard McCoy, another of the crowd. "I already know. I'm the editor of the *News-Democrat*."

My old Rotax will run on anything, from British four star leaded petrol to 100ll avgas or lead-free auto fuel. But I'm not sure if I had been that Piper pilot that I wouldn't just have flown on to Nashville to refuel there. I wondered just how fresh the fuel was, it was obvious that Humphreys County didn't sell a lot of it. There was not a single aircraft tied down on the apron. Apparently there had been a dispute with the man who owned and worked in the hangar and he had refused to quit, so all the aircraft owners had departed instead.

Tim Simmons invited me for Sunday lunch with his folks, "good old Southern-style cooking". There were so many of us we had two sittings, men first. I wasn't objecting, I had skipped breakfast and it was more than a day since I had had a proper meal. Afterwards, Tim took me on a quick tour of the power station where he worked and the huge mounds of ash piled around it.

On our way back I was getting worried about the fading light and anxious to get back in the air. I was about to fly off the edge of the Atlanta sectional chart and wanted the morale boost of packing a second map away. From the outline of the US on the back, I would then have four more sectionals to cross, I would be a third of the way across the country.

As we sat at a railway crossing, a huge tanker train rumbled by at walking speed. My frustration must have shown. "A few years back a train derailed and there was an explosion that destroyed half the town," Tim said. "Now there are very strict speed limits."

I was back in the air, following the same railway tracks, just after 7pm, landing 40 minutes later 23 miles away in Benson, just on the edge of the Memphis sectional. I was now one third of the way across the States and preparing to head down the Mississippi and pick up my original planned route.

I was about to put up my tent when a retired doctor and his wife who had just landed offered a bed for the night. He had to get up early, he said. What he did not say was he lived 30 minutes from the airfield and early was 5am. Most nights in Scotland I don't get to bed before then and now I was up at that time two days in a row!

The 6:20 departure was my earliest flight ever, although it is rumoured (rumoured in case the British Civil Aviation Authority read this, microlight pilots are not allowed to operate at night) that I once flew at 1am in the Scottish Highlands.

The plan had been to get round the Memphis zone by heading south down the Tennessee River via Parson and Savannah to Corinth. But Flight Service put paid to that with forecasts of south westerly winds. I hadn't topped up at Humphreys County and it was too early to fuel up at Benson, so 40 miles into wind to Scott Field at Parsons might just be too much.

It turned out I could have gone south, the wind aloft had a northerly component so it took 50 minutes to cover the 20 miles to Carroll County. I unpacked the Pink Panther, took out the belly tank and poured the three gallons left in it into the main tank, and then strapped everything back in. A couple of miles west I could pick up the railway line and follow it south-west to Humboldt.

Of course, by 8:20am the wind had swung round, so it was right on the nose as I headed south-west. Within minutes of take-off, a look at the GPS confirmed my suspicions that I might not have enough fuel for the 35 miles leg, so I kept a touch to the north of the railway and headed for Gibson County. The 24 miles took 70 minutes and I was down to my last gallon when I landed.

At first glance, Gibson was just another small field. But in the grass next to the ramp was a small stone tablet carved with a picture of an autogyro, the name Mark Gilbert Justice May 1, 1927 - Jan 8 1988 and the message:

This story will be told many times in many ways. The truth is he saved my life. As he died a hero. Mark, I shall be eternally thankful.
May you fly with the eagles forever.

Glen C Pery

I was told that Mark had taken up an autogyro built by Glen for its flight test and was killed when it crashed. No-one would say whether it had been pilot error, poor design, structural failure or one of the hundreds of other factors that can cause a catastrophe. I guess the plaque was intended to say it all.

It was something to think about as I caught up with my sleep waiting for evening when the Class D restriction at McKellar Sipes was lifted. Despite Russell fitting a new aerial at Rutherfordton, I still had no confidence in my radio and wanted to avoid controlled airspace whenever possible.

10

Mississippi Meander

*"To put your life in danger from
time to time ... breeds a
saneness in dealing with
day-to-day trivialities."*

Nevil Shute, *Slide Rule*

The lack of reliable communications made me decide to get away from McKellar Sipes before the tower opened at 6:30. The Pink Panther was wheeled into a plush hangar with corporate jets for company while I pitched my tent outside the flight service station.

Carla at the FBO lent me a car to go down the road for a roast pork sandwich at the local mart. When I returned the keys, she offered me a coffee and then told me about the ghostly goings on around the hangars. The previous Christmas, they had decorated their tree with musical lights that switched themselves on and played tunes in the evening even though the power was off.

Electricians checking the circuits could find nothing to explain it, and the guys on the line, Greg and Jim, said it was just one of many weird and unexplained things they had experienced. The airfield was built on what had been a major battleground against the Indians and their spirits are thought to linger still. Though why they would want to interfere with a Christmas tree no-one could say. The first of the three questions I was asked was, of course: Have you ever seen the Loch Ness monster?

The engine played its usual hard-to-start game in the morning and as I radioed to taxi for take-off, the FSS told me I had two minutes before the tower opened.

At 6:30 on the dot, as I was doing my pre-take-off checks before moving onto the runway, McKellar ground called to ask the "aircraft on taxiway" to identify itself. I just could not believe they hadn't been listening out for the few minutes before the shift officially started.

The controller did not seem to know what to do with an aircraft that was so slow that it took a couple of minutes after take-off before I could call clear of the airfield boundary – it was quite a long runway and the wind was strong.

I stopped off at Whitehurst at 7:30 am to change fuel tanks. Just as I was restarting the engine, a car pulled up with the airfield manager, Dave Perrin, who said he had seen me fly over and thought I might be wanting my tank topped up. A few minutes later, his partner, Steve Aldred, turned up – an Englishman from Lancashire, the county where my aircraft was made.

He was very interested in the Pink Panther and, strangely enough, his brother lived just around the corner from the Mainair factory. With his aviation experience, I suggested that if he wanted to get a trike he buy a bare airframe from Mainair and then add the instruments, engine and prop in America to cut the costs. Basically, I found that whatever something was in pounds sterling back in Scotland, it was the same in dollars in the States, but the exchange rate meant that I got $16 for every £10, so there could be quite a saving. It also meant, of course, that British trike manufacturers found it very difficult to sell in the US.

A few minutes later, it was off to Holly Springs, 20 miles west of Memphis and near Elvis's birthplace. Bad weather was forecast, so I got the machine tied down and went into town for lunch with Bill and Buddy, a couple of guys who were working on their plane at the flying club hangar.

They greeted me saying: "Welcome to the worst little strip in Mississippi."

I had to admit, with a crosswind the rotor off the trees made it a little exciting coming in. We stood for a couple of minutes and watched a Cessna 150 doing touch and goes, its wings waggling as the rotor caught it.

Bill and Buddy were pals from Vietnam. Bill had thought I was an Australian at first, bringing back happy memories of training Kiwis and Ozzies in anti-submarine reconnaissance. Apparently, while a bunch were in California in the late 60s the Australian prime minister died and the Australian embassy sent enough booze to the airmen to hold a wake that lasted a week. Ever since, Bill has been trying to repay his debt of gratitude to any Australian he meets.

I told them Joe Kittinger's Vietnam tale from Sun'n Fun: "Pearl beer was 10c a bottle and there were hundreds of thousands of empties cluttering up the base so I loaded up the bomb bay and dumped 10,000 of the SoB's on a road in North Vietnam! I reckoned it wouldn't be too good for their tires.

"The crew chief didn't like it, the plane stank of beer for days. But I did it once a week for six months."

I spent the night on a sofa in the clubhouse, thinking as I fell asleep how cheap flying here was compared to back home.

A notice on the clubhouse board read:

Flying instruction:

40 hours for aircraft at $33 an hour ...$1,320

20 hours with instructor at $15 an hour ...$300

Flight check ride for FAA ...$100

Club dues for 1 year (includes loan of training videos) $50

Total .... $1,770 dollars

In Scotland, you would be lucky to get 40 hours for less than the equivalent of $6,000. At some airports the landing fee alone is almost $15, so a bunch of touch and goes can empty your wallet pretty fast.

Bill and Buddy were adamant that there was nothing in Holly Springs worth noting. Later I wondered about this, since everyone seemed to know Holly Springs. It turned out it had a Vortac navigation beacon, so made a handy turning point.

With no breakfast, it was an early take-off just after dawn south-west to the Mississippi river. The forecast was not good, but then again the local winds were not that bad and there was plenty of flat ground around. As Greg joked in an e-mail, it's all downhill from here to New Orleans.

As I flew across the flat fields I could hear the chatter on the radio about thunderstorms to the north. Although it was overcast, the sky to the south was much lighter, so I pressed on. Ahead of me there was an airfield called Selfs marked on the sectional. I could always find a motel there if the worst came to the worst, I thought. I did not look forward to spending a thunderstorm in a tent.

It turned out that Selfs was just a short strip in

the middle of a field with a one-plane hangar. Keeping an eye on the weather, I stopped to chat for a moment with a black farmer who was ploughing the fields. Another ex-services man, he had planned to settle in Arizona or New Mexico, but then decided to stay near his parents.

He wanted to know if I was married. He had been once, he said. When he heard I wasn't, he said he understood how I could afford the trip.

"Yo better off keeping animals than a wife," he told me. "At best, a woman spends all your money on hersel'; at worst, she spends it on 'nother man."

The sky to the north suddenly seemed to get much darker, so I said a hurried goodbye and set out on a quick hop down the road to Cleveland. It was actually a 45 mile leg, the distance from Glasgow to Edinburgh, cities back home that are world's apart. Yet now that I had flown 2,000 miles, with another 2,000 to go, distance had taken on a new meaning and it seemed like nothing.

Once in the air, I could see the sky darkening to the west as well. There were thunderclouds from just south of Memphis sweeping right round to the north. I pulled on speed to make sure I kept well away as I headed for the sectional's southern edge.

After a dozen or so miles, I was getting clear of the storms. But the atmosphere failed to lighten as I came across a prison complex so large it was marked on the aviation chart.

Months later in Edinburgh, I learned just what I had flown past when one of our American correspondents, Jonathan Ledgard, filed this story:

> Parchman, Mississippi's state prison, is sprawled out over 16,000 acres of flat farmland in the Mississippi Delta. On this golden autumn day in the land of the Blues it doesn't seem a bad place. Even the watchtower guards are amiable.
>
> As one drives deeper into the facility however, the mood darkens. There, suddenly, is death row – the omega point for the most heinous crimes in Mississippi. It looks forbidding, a grim blockhouse, hemmed in by floodlights and high barbed wire.
>
> Further up is a constellation of cellblocks, each isolated by acres of untilled fields: a cellblock for prisoners with HIV, a secure cellblock to protect sex-offenders and snitches.
>
> At the far end of Parchman is an unprepossessing barracks – the RID (Regimented Inmates Discipline) programme. Mississippi judges have the option of sending non-violent offenders here. If they pass RID's rigorous six month military-style bootcamp their jail terms are waived. This is where the debris of the drug war washes up.
>
> Parchman now houses 5,500 of Mississippi's 14,000 prisoners, up from only 1,200 in the 1970s. The state has the highest incarceration rate in the Western world. A new law promises further to swell the numbers. All criminals – no matter how fine their behaviour inside – must now serve out 85 per cent of their sentence. New inmates – most of them young kids involved in the drug economy – continue to arrive; fewer are leaving.

The problems are not specific to Mississippi; 80 per cent of the prisoners are inside for a drug or alcohol related crime, 75 per cent of prisoners are black. The trend is towards younger, more violent offenders. Since crack-cocaine arrived in Mississippi the prison population has grown 130 per cent. Sociologists have identified a new breed of criminals and called them super-predators.

"They are completely amoral and without fear of death," says one prison officer. "They'll kill without a passing thought. The only thing we can do is to isolate them."

The governor's mansion in Jackson feels a long way from Parchman and the "super-predators" prowling maximum security cells. There, spreading himself on an elegant 18th century chair, Governor Kirk Fordice holds forth on Mississippi's economic successes and social ills. Mr Fordice is a businessman by trade and a religious right bully by disposition. He is also a proud Scottish-American who likes to begin: "We Scots think like this ..." when justifying his tough-love ideas.

This is his second term in office and he is lucky to be alive. A year ago he overturned his car at 120mph. "The source of the crime problem is unsupported, unwanted children," he says, speaking fast, like ammo popping off. "Call me a Scot if you like, but I think children should be born into a loving family, not the result of hormones in a car back seat."

The governor believes in privatising almost everything, including the prisons. He also wants a return to traditional values. "I brought back striped uniforms for prisoners to teach them some shame."

Almost everyone in Mississippi, including leftist Democrats, agree with this, saying the main problem is that the young have lost their moral compass.

The gloom, literal and metaphorical, was soon well behind me. The Mississippi river and Cleveland airfield now clearly visible ahead. The runway was directly north-south, with a fine, broad, east-west taxiway at the southern end. The airfield advised a 10 to 12 mph wind from the east, so I requested to land on the taxiway.

"I'll have to speak to the airfield manager," the lady on the radio said.

"Go ahead, Cleveland. My maximum crosswind component is 10 mph," I replied. "I'll orbit awaiting a response."

A few minutes later, a man's voice said: "Cleveland calling ultralight.

"The active runway is three-five. Do you copy? The taxiway is not to be used. The active runway is three-five."

"That's copied. Ultralight Golf Mike Whisky X-ray Uniform turning downwind for three-five Cleveland. Out."

I came in 50ft to the left of the runway and turned to land diagonally across it at the last minute, rolling out onto a runoff. With the wind, my landing distance was only 50 or 60ft. The aviation department of the local university had a hangar there and a bunch of them gave me a big wave as I taxied past. I suppose they must have heard my conversation on the hangar radio.

I expected a frosty welcome at the FBO but no-one mentioned a thing. They were obviously busy but I was efficiently refuelled. A busy airport is a good sign, I think, so I asked if someone could examine my wiring because the radio did not seem to be getting any charge.

One of the mechanics, Pete, said he would have a quick look, but with it being a Monday they were "real busy" with problems that had built up over the weekend and I might have "to wait awhiles". When they got round to me, it ended up taking Pete and another chap a good half hour to check the circuits out and get things sorted.

One of their major businesses was rebuilding Stearman biplanes – one was almost finished in a nearby hanger and looked better than new. I would have been frightened to fly it for fear of a fly marking the paintwork.

When the job was finished, Pete handed me his card and said: "There you are. That's it sorted. No charge."

Those restored biplanes are $149,000 each. If I ever make a million, Pete Jones, owner of Air Repair at Cleveland, will be getting a call. Judging from the gracious way he treated a passing ultralighter, there won't be many other aircraft as painstakingly and perfectly restored.

I never saw or heard from the airfield manager and the lady on the radio, it was as if they were from a different airfield.

Lake Village sounded like a pretty place for a stop to celebrate crossing the mighty Mississippi and the chance to add another state, Arkansas, to my logbook. Unfortunately Lake Village was just a crop dusting strip, with the canary yellow plane taking off and landing every four or five minutes. The guys busy reloading the hoppers just shouted at me to help myself to a can of soda from the office and went back to their work, so it was back in the air to Byerley, Louisiana. Three states in a day, I really felt like I was travelling now.

I waited until the duster had filled up again before I taxied to take-off. By the time I was in the air, he was swinging down to land again. These guys were quick, there was no messing about and no circuit procedure. It was straight in and straight back out again. I decided to add bright yellow planes to my list of people to give way to.

Thunderclouds to the north, thunderclouds springing up to the west ... and the east. I was glad to be following the river south. As it twisted from one side to another I decided to head straight to Byerley, Lake Providence, letting the river weave underneath me.

My main concern was to get to an airfield before the storm broke overhead. Landing in a field would not have been difficult, there were grass strips and dirt roads everywhere you look, it just wouldn't have been much fun. The big problem was that I had not had anything to eat since my late lunch the previous afternoon with Bill and Buddy and I was beginning to feel more than hungry.

Byerley was home to the grand-daddy of dusters, Steve Geunard. A former dive-bomber pilot, Steve had run a crop dusting business for 40 years – his longevity proof that he knows what he is doing – before selling out. His office at the field was like a museum of aviation and, hunger ignored, I spent a couple of hours that afternoon chatting to him and some of his pals who had spotted the Pink Panther's distinctive wing sticking up in the air.

I was told that Steve had bought an old plantation house back in 1940 when the shores of Lake Providence were virtually undeveloped. The air-field is named after his uncle, Frank Byerley, who learned to fly in the First World War – although he never flew in combat – and there is a picture of him next to a Lockheed Vega. Special taken in 1929 that hangs in the middle of Steve's office wall.

Steve's son is a pilot too, and is rebuilding a Stearman, the type his father was taught to fly in. He thought his son had paid a fortune for a pile of junk ... until I told him what a fully-restored version would cost at Cleveland.

The thunderclouds continued to build, so we hangared the Pink Panther and Dan Osbourne, a cotton trader, and his wife Mary offered to put me up at their home. I went off in Dan's truck to find something to eat and when I returned Steve had left a note offering to let me camp out in his office. Like McKellar-Sipes, I think it might have been haunted too ... but with friendly ghosts from the golden days of aviation.

Dan's generosity was all the greater when I discovered he was due to go into hospital a week later for a serious operation.

Here's an example of how crazy crop dusters are. Talking of a field where the power company had erected 60ft poles along one side, Steve admitted it had made it a little more difficult to dust, although you could fly under the wires.

"You really have to watch it when the crops grow a little, though," he said.

"Not only does that eat into the space below the wires, but the hotter weather at that time of the year makes the wires stretch and sag a little too."

A headwind the next morning made the flight down the Mississippi to Vicksburg Regional take 50 minutes. Vicksburg, across the river, is where, in 1894, the first Coca-Cola was bottled. I checked to see which brand of cola their soda machine sold.

Tommy Grant, the airfield manager, was keen to point out Vicksburg's attractions ... antebellum homes from before the Civil War, including Grey Oaks, a Southern mansion built as a plantation home in Port Gibson, Mississippi, in 1834 and then bought, dismantled and moved to Vicksburg in 1940 with its facade redesigned as a replica of Tara from *Gone with the Wind*.

It is now on the Bed and Breakfast circuit. Back home, B&Bs are cheap accommodation at around $30 a night. On the Mississippi, they are historic mansions costing from $90 a night up.

Roach rooms for me.

Back in the air, I realised my fuel consumption seemed a little high. Fighting the headwind I had been pulling the bar in and pushing the throttle forward to increase speed, but at 50 per cent above normal, fuel usage was excessive.

A precautionary landing at Tensal Parish failed to find any obvious cause. Then a pre-flight check revealed a broken exhaust mount. I was on a deserted airfield, with no telephone, I had not yet had breakfast and it was nearly noon.

A bit of wire scavenged from a hangar floor helped to tie on the radiator and it was a 40 minute flight to Natchez. The map showed three runways, so I reckoned there would be a mechanic there. The only other thing I knew about Natchez was that Jack Lemmon implied at the start of the film *The Apartment* that it was nowhere special when his character, CC Baxter, of Consolidated Life, says: "On

November 1, 1959, the population of New York City was 8,042,783. If, assuming an average height of 5ft 7, they were laid head to toe they would form a line stretching from Times Square to Karachi, Pakistan. Our home office has 31,259 employees, which is more than the population of ... Natchez, Mississippi."

Of course, since I was guzzling the gas and had wired on my radiator with a bit of scrap, the flat rice fields gave way to forest. Rather than take the winding route along the river and risk running out of fuel I flew straight along the bearing and hoped nothing would fall off while I was over the trees.

Clinton Pomeroy, director of aviation at Natchez-Adams County Airport, came out to welcome me. The mechanic was with the fire department for the day, but Clinton telephoned some local ultralight pilots and the consensus was that the air filter had got clogged up.

Eddie Thorpe, owner of Natchez Cycle Supply, sourced a filter and arranged for overnight delivery. Eddie had flown ultralights ten years ago when the craze first swept America until he hit some power lines. He was in hospital for months.

That night, I went to Natchez-under-the-hill, the area down by the river. Journalistic instinct found the bar with 50 cent beers. As I tried to charm a Southern belle with my Scottish accent, another guy kept butting in. As it turned out, we both got the brush-off when her boyfriend arrived.

Tim Chesnee is not your typical American oilman. Apart from anything else, he has a small hat and a small truck and doesn't smoke cigars.

As we ate tamales in the only bar still open, he suggested taking my welding problem to Percy's Radiator Service. So, in the morning it was off in the airfield truck to collect my filter from Eddie ($50 included a 10 buck freight charge but was still cheaper than back home) and hand in the radiator.

At the airfield, the local press in the shape of photographer Brett Duke was waiting. Brett was renting an apartment from Tim and, like the good newspaper man that he is, took me off to a bar immediately the pictures were taken. So began another night of alcoholic shame "under-the-hill", with Brett and Tim, their girlfriends Adriana and Vickie, and a crowd of others.

Just one street is left under the bluff at Natchez, where once there had been a thriving town serving the riverboat trade. The rest has been swept away by the river. In the early days, gamblers were accepted as an essential part of the local economy, but the tide turned as their notoriety grew and by the 1830s the *Natchez Courier* proclaimed that their presence was driving down property values. As each settlement along the river became a proper township, the gamblers were the first to be ordered out, if they were lucky. At Vicksburg, in July 1835, vigilante settlers publicly strung up five gamblers.

The barman told me this was typical as towns like Natchez, Vicksburg and Memphis forged their identity. Law and order yielded to the making of money. One visitor's diary recorded that Vicksburg was a town "run mad with speculation. They do business in a kind of frenzy. Money is scarce but credit is plenty". Money was scarce for me too, so I didn't join the girls when they crossed the street to visit the riverboat casino, a replica paddlesteamer moored at the riverbank.

There was bad news the next day. Percy Marion Pritchard (echoes of John Wayne here) had not realised my radiator was made of aluminium, which they couldn't weld, and the Memorial Day Weekend was starting. It was an outside chance, but we tried Scott's Welding.

The lads were all in working on a rush job, but Dana promised he would come in on the holiday Monday to fix it. So it was down to Lake St John with the girls for two days of beer, barbeques and bathing.

Bliss.

The lakeside house was home to Vicky's pal Cindy Lou, who was staying with her mother, Miss Betty. They could not understand why I preferred to sleep in the tent in the garden and listen to the noises of nature than the hum of air-conditioning. I was wondering if there were bugs they hadn't told me about when, as I drifted off to sleep, the tent shook as something was flung into the side of it and I felt an animal's breath pressing through the fabric behind my head. After a moment of terror and confusion, I realised the cat was perched on the tent roof and taunting the family dog.

On Monday afternoon Tim and I changed the sparkplugs, fitted the new airfilter and repaired radiator and took the Pink Panther up for a shake-down flight. With evening storms forecast, I planned to spend the night in town and leave at dawn. Back under-the-hill, we sat outside watching the lightning storm drift south down the river. It was to continue until 2:30 the following afternoon.

Back home, we often dismiss work hassles by saying: What the heck, it is only tomorrow's fish and chip wrapper. The Mississippi version must be tamale wrapper, for the mayor of under-the-hill served us our late night snack wrapped in copies of *The Natchez Democrat* with Duke's photograph of me on the front page: Scot stranded in Natchez.

But not for long. I had decided that following the storm down to New Orleans was a bad idea. Despite the fabulous hospitality of my new friends, I was also impatient to get going towards the west. Texas beckoned and stories of its size made me wonder if I'd ever get across it. The weather charts were also showing the midday temperatures there were beginning to exceed a 100 degrees. Maybe I had left it too late in the year to fly there?

11

The Sun Has Riz ...

"Unlike the boundaries of the sea by the shorelines, the 'ocean of air' laps at the border of every state, city, town and home throughout the world."

Welch Pogue

As the rain stopped at Natchez airport, Clinton asked if I was getting going. I had been there for six days and the record for being stranded was a full week set the previous year by an elderly couple trying to get to Ohio from New Orleans who were forced to land as the weather closed in.

I had spent the morning sleeping in a dark corner of the hangar until the storm stopped. After lunch I was still unsure whether the bad weather had gone far enough south, but decided to press on since my course was due west. After take-off, I did a couple of orbits before crossing the mile-wide Mississippi, looking at the weather, looking at my chart, wondering whether it might be better to head for one of the airfields a little bit to the north.

I decided to go for it. An hour later I was in Pollock, some sixty miles across Louisiana. All through the flight I could hear hissing as the storm cells to my left fired off thunderbolts, yet just a few miles to the north were clear blue skies.

Fortunately, the airfield at Pollock was right below the band of white cloud that fringed the black mass to the south. I landed to find it was deserted. I taxied around looking for signs of life and eventually stopped in front of the fuel pump. A hanger door was unlocked and I used the rest room and was about to make a telephone call from the pilot's lounge when a voice rang out: "Who's there. Come on out!"

Two men had pulled up in a truck and seemed very suspicious of my intentions, insisting that the door had been locked. I calmed them down and finally persuaded them to sell me some fuel.

Just two or three miles to the south, the sky was flecked with thunderflashes, but Flight Service promised they were heading south at 15 mph and that I had a tailwind below 1,000 ft. So I decided not to risk overstaying my welcome and hurried off for Nachitoches. Back at Rockwood in Tennessee I had been told that one of the main uses for many remote airfields was for anti-drug patrols, where spotter aircraft were used to detect cannabis plantations. The reception committee at Pollock made me wonder if that airfield had found a less legitimate role.

This part of the world is also the home of the Bowie knife. Even before his death at the Alamo, Bowie had a reputation as an adventurer; he fought Indians, searched for Spanish gold and married into the Mexican aristocracy. But his knife-fighting reputation was established at the Sandbar Duel above Natchez in 1827 when, although severely wounded, Bowie killed another man with a "big knife". And so began the legend. His obituary in the *Democratic Telegraph and Texas Register* read: "He was brave without fear and generous beyond precedent; and though he had faults, and gigantic ones too, he atoned for all the errors of a stormy life by the splendour of his death."

Safely back in the air, I plotted my course for the next airfield, Nachitoches. Apart from helping tell what other traffic is about, the handy thing about the radio, when it works, is that you can hear how to pronounce a place. Otherwise how would I have known to say Knacka-dish?

It was only 7:15pm when I arrived and there was an hour of daylight left and just 60 miles to go to get across the rest of Louisiana and into Texas. But the last hour of dodging thunderstorms had made me glad to be safe on the ground, with a hangar for the Pink Panther.

It was a tempting thought to cross a state in a day, but the thought of a good meal and a comfortable bed to set me up for the Lone Star state was too much.

Next morning, things were slow to get going, partly due to ground mist. And there was no taxi service. Eventually, a lift from the motel owner got me to the airfield ready for a late start.

There was a little entertainment when a twin-engined job bringing a sheriff in for talks with his local counterpart got lost on the airfield and kept going down dead-end taxiways. I had a good look at an aerial photograph of the field before I started taxiing.

With a 1,200 ft cloudbase, the flight to Center, Texas, was uneventful. I probably got pretty close to marginal VFR as I crossed a lake and then the river marking the Texas boundary. Being close to cloud can be daunting, but it is comforting to have a little height in case the engine quits.

At Center, there was a little strip with Xs on it, showing it was not to be used, that was right into wind. But the main runway was so wide that a diagonal landing achieved the same effect. Allan, the airfield manager, was justifiably proud of it and the parallel taxiway that was the width of the old runway. Three and a half million dollars worth – all because, others said, some well-connected people jet in for hunting trips.

I got back from lunch at a local cafe, to discover Allan had called the local paper, *The Light and Champion*, to tell them about me. Mattew Postins came down to interview me and take pictures. His front page article ended:

> "Part of this flight is in the spirit of the early days of aviation," Mr MacKinnon says. "There's no inflight movie or a flight attendant in the back with a drink for me."
>
> Armed with his quick wit and a map of Texas that took up two pages, Mr MacKinnon prepared to head for his next destination, Palestine. Noticing the size of Texas, he remembered an old joke.
>
> "Well, there's the Texan farmer who stops to talk to the Scottish farmer. The Scottish farmer has just a few acres for his sheep. The Texan farmer says: 'Back home, I can get in my truck and drive all day and still not make it around my farm.' The Scottish farmer replies: 'Yeah, I've got a truck like that too.' So that's my Texas joke."
>
> What Mr MacKinnon is doing is no joke, as he sets out to finish what his Irish ancestor started almost 100 years ago.

Allan was an ex-police officer and completely against President Clinton's gun control plans. As we whiled away the afternoon in the single-roomed clubhouse cum office, he brought out a copy of *Shotgun News* – which appeared to have adverts for every type of gun in it except shotguns – and described how even guns that were outlawed could be made up from components bought separately.

In his eyes, this seemed to be proof that attempts at gun control were bad, rather than evidence that the laws were badly drawn up. He just could not understand the idea that police in Britain did not carry firearms and that we were proposing a handgun ban in the wake of the tragedy at Dunblane in which a madman gunned down a class of primary schoolchildren and their teacher.

As storms were forecast, Allan found me hangar space and said I was welcome to sleep on the sofa. His wife was away for a few days and he didn't know how to cook, so he was going round to his daughter's for a decent meal that night, he explained, otherwise he would have invited me to stay at his place.

As it turned out, the weather suddenly cleared at 5:50pm and it was what would be described back home as a beautiful summer's evening. Flight Service said the radar showed it was the same all along my route, so I rushed to load up the Pink Panther and make the most of it. I was well aware of the tradition saying which reflects the state's size: The sun has riz, the sun has set, and we ain't outta Texas yet.

Ninety five minutes later and I was 92 miles further across Texas at Palestine, home of a Nasa balloon launching facility. It was 20 minutes before eight and the FBO was closed. At Mexia, 49 miles away, my directory said there was a 24-hour office.

After a few minutes of hesitation, I swapped from sunglasses to ordinary spectacles, changed tanks, squeezed the rubber bulb to force the fuel through and tried to start her up. As the minutes ticked by, the engine just would not fire. Finally, I swapped back to the rear tank and she started first time. I then switched to the belly tank and with the engine now running the pump sucked the fuel through without a problem. I now had 40 minutes before sunset to cover 50 miles.

As I pulled the bar in and pushed down on the throttle, my groundspeed hit 87mph. A new record.

There was no traffic on the radio, but I had been told that Mexia, was pronounced Mey-hay-ah so I felt people would at least understand which airfield's pattern I was joining.

The town was established in 1871, and named after the Mexican General Jose Antonio Mexia whose family donated the land. The general first served under the dictator Santa Anna, but later joined a rebellion against him. When it failed, he died before a firing squad.

Right on the button of dusk, I joined downwind at Mexia. As I called out my turn on to base, a car drew up on the road to watch so I playfully pulled on some speed by diving a little towards it before hauling the Pink Panther round for a short final.

In the hangar, one chap asked if I had not been a little low on the approach. "Speed is height," I replied. "And height is safety," the car driver, who had just pulled up on the ramp, muttered with more than a hint of irony.

The operation at Mexia seemed pretty busy, with a hangar filled with twins. But a space was found for the Pink Panther and over the next few minutes each of the mechanics offered to give me a lift into town. It was great to experience the spirit that enables people after a long and hard day's work to think of others first.

The "it's a small world" syndrome struck again with Gastone Rossato, an Italian working at the airfield, who was being met by his wife Carol, an Englishwoman from Sussex. The next day, Gastone arranged for me to be interviewed by the local newspaper, then took me for a flight over the airfield to take pictures of a pretend aircraft crash organised by the local fire brigade. I can't say it didn't make me feel uneasy.

As the skies grew darker, the Pink Panther was pushed back into the hangar's shelter. It looked like another night in Mexia, so I had a quick interview with Carl Haddick of KYCX FM News, who has also launched a local internet access service.

As he e-mailed me later: "You were quite the talk of Mexia. Our conversation ran twice on the local FM station, and you were prominently featured on the front page of the *Mexia Daily News.*"

But I don't think Anna Nicole Smith, the model and billionaire's plaything, needs worry that I'll hog the local limelight. Born in Mexia in 1967, Vickie Lynn Hogan worked as a topless dancer in Houston before becoming a Playboy Playmate of the Year in 1992. But what really raised eyebrows was her marriage in 1994 to J Howard Marshall, an 89-year-old wheelchair-bound billionaire, who died a happy man just a year later. His heirs claimed, successfully, that he couldn't have been in full possession of his facilities when he married, so Nicole "only" received about $2 million.

Eric and D'Eva Redding, former Playboy scouts, wrote in their book *The Great Big Beautiful Plastic Doll* that her fame owes more to the surgeon's skills than mother nature's blessing. "Anna is quoted as telling a fellow dancer who wanted to touch her breasts: 'Feel them puppies all you want. You're looking at $14,000 worth of work here. Hell, I could have bought myself a truck for what these damn things costs.' She claims they were a gift from God."

What I found truly amazing was that in a town of just 7,161 souls, not one would tell me anything of substance about Anna Nicole's early life.

Gastone came by the hangar as Carl was interviewing me and said he would be back in 30 minutes. Of course, the weather then cleared up into another beautiful evening.

I waited an hour and then decided I had to press on. Hillsboro was 48 miles away and I made it in 40 minutes, getting there just before dark. For the first time, I had noted the numbers of local hotels. But at the airfield there was an empty hangar with a broken door and a beautiful new office with a telephone to the local police station which issued the security lock combination in exchange for my aircraft registration number and pilot's licence number. It was the first time I have ever had to give my licence number to anyone. Dinner that night was corn chips and jalapeno cheddar sauce, with the lightening flashing in the sky.

The storm's flickers brought back memories of Natchez and I felt homesick for my new friends. Even the mayor, Larry L "Butch" Brown had found time out from his election campaign to talk to me in his office and present me with a book of historic photographs of Mississippi steamboats inscribed: "Thank you for your interest in our community – please use this to remind you of your stay in Natchez." His rival's slogan was: The Honest Candidate. Now who would vote for a politician who described himself like that?

Butch and his father had visited Scotland and stayed in Inverlochy Castle, one of the country's most exclusive hotels. Mary Bisland, a friend of Tim's had also stayed there on a trip to the homeland. It made me realise there was probably a lot more money in Natchez than appearances first suggested.

Tim later sent this e-mail via my Web site:

"Well, we have been to Lake St. John several times since you left and they still mention your name. Quite a memory you left, and the dent in the ground where you tread near the hammock!

"People have begun to return to the Under-the-Hill saloon now that you are safely away; you really had the place emptied out there for several days, adding to the mystique I suppose. Such a dangerous fellow, they must have thought.

"And the newspaper story, that one did it. Little old ladies strolled around town for days carrying their copy with them, should they see the little Scottie. Word was that some didn't believe the whole thing, like doubting the moon landings, and others wanted to be a stowaway on your adventure, and here's the topper. Rumor had it that you were to be added to certain TRUSTS, making you one of them ..."

As I fell asleep, I dreamt of the days when Mary's ancestors, who were originally Bilslands, used to send one of the family home to Scotland to sell each year's crop from the plantation and visit relations. The whole trip would take 12 months, by which time another member would be ready to leave and maintain the connections with the old country over the generations.

The old mansion, the last link with those gracious, unhurried days, had just been sold, Mary told me. To avoid the row which had split so many families along the Mississippi, Mary and her sisters agreed to take turns in choosing things that they wanted, and if any sister raised an objection the item was to be sold and the money shared. What fascinated me were the estate accounts, going back almost 200 years, detailing the price of slaves and how little they were paid after emancipation. The archives are now in a local museum.

12

Stormy Weather

"Imagine a locomotive that has left its track, and is climbing up in the air right toward you – a locomotive without any wheels ... but with white wings instead ... a locomotive made of aluminium."

Amos Ives Root, on witnessing the first circle flown

Just after dawn, I was back in the air for Clerk Field at Stephensville. Lovely big runways, but a dip in the ground before the threshold of the one into wind, so a fast approach. I cut through the expected sink, then at the intersection of the two runways .... whoah!! Time for my third go-around in the USA.

Next time, I came in high – why should I bother landing on the numbers at the start of a 3,000 feet runway? I was glad I had, there really was strange air lurking over the first 500ft of that runway.

After refuelling, I went for the usual late breakfast/early lunch. That day's *Dallas Morning News* had a full page feature on a recently-closed fashion store that began in the mid-1960s "as an outpost of hippie style so groovy even Jimmy Page and Robert plant were customers". But it ensured itself more than a footnote in Texan history by opening a hair salon with a woman hairdresser cutting men's hair.

"When the barbers' association found out what we were doing, they went to the sheriff's department and filed a complaint. They said only cosmet-ologists could cut women's hair and only barbers could cut men's. Our attorney filed papers saying that that law was unconstitutional," Charles Bolton, the store's founder said.

A three-judge panel agreed and the 12th District Court in New Orleans threw out an appeal. "Then the barbers went to the Supreme Court, and they knocked down the law totally."

Back at the airfield, I found John Darby and Arnie Schecht sitting on a bench outside the office enjoying the sunshine. After warning me of bad weather on the way, and finding an empty hangar for the Pink Panther, they invited me to the EAA Chapter 986 meeting near Dallas.

John had built an RV6, named Teddytoo after a favourite Yorkshire terrier that had died just two months before the machine made its first flight

Arnie had rebuilt a Piper PA22/20 and had taken it down to the Kerrville airshow. Someone walking around took a good look at, made a remark about a spot on the leading edge that the paint had missed and said they had "never seen anything like it". Arnie was not sure what to say, his aircraft was only at the show because he had flown there in it. A few weeks later, he got a plaque in the post as reserve champion, contemporary classic. I presume it was for his machine, but he and John were such gentlemen they deserved a prize in their own right. In the nicest possible way, they made me thing of a flying version of the Odd Couple.

After noting this on my web site, I got the following e-mail from John:

"We have come to the conclusion that you mean we both have the desirable traits of Felix and Oscar. Our wives say it is only the undesirable traits of each! An aside. You remember that Arnie and I are both a little into age. He is older than I. Didn't realise the difference until the other day. We were walking along, a frog jumped up and hit his leg. He kicked it away. The frog kept coming back and jumping up. After the fourth or fifth time, Arnie picked it up. When he did, the frog began to talk: "I am really a beautiful girl. If you kiss me I will turn into a voluptuous loving woman and take care of all your needs with my beautiful body for life. Just kiss me."

Arnie just put the frog in his pocket. I was shocked, I asked him what he was doing.

He replied: "At my age, I'm more interested in a talking frog."

The EAA meeting was in a private estate called Pecan Plantation, with its own security guards, boating lake, golf course and airstrip. Every house by the airstrip had to have its own hangar ... this is the good life, Texas style.

With the guest speaker prevented from travelling because of the weather, I gave a short talk about my flight and handed out cards. Many later e-mailed with their good wishes.

Back at Clerk, the winds that had blown the roofs off houses in Dallas suddenly calmed to a 10 mph tailwind, so it was back in the air. Could I make Abilene by dusk?

The radio still did not seem to be transmitting, so the controlled airspace of Abilene Regional, was out. But I could still receive, and their air traffic information service was broadcasting a report 12mph winds out of the east, meaning a stronger crosswind than the safety placard allows if I was to land on the north-south strip marked at nearby Elmdale Airpark.

It was something to think about as I flew past Eastland and Cisco, both with north-south strips. Where to stay was another question, prompted by my Flight-trivia map which highlighted Cisco as the place where, when Conrad Hilton couldn't find a place to sleep in 1919, he bought the Mobley Hotel, which then became the first in his empire.

As Elmdale came into view, problems were solved. Someone had cut a crosswind strip in the grass. An overhead flight to eye it up and a quick turn over the fence and I was down, landing on the first half in case there was a ridge where it crossed the main runway.

I taxied up to the empty office next to the fuel pumps and considered changing tanks and heading for Avenger. Fortunately I didn't, or I would have missed what became one of my favourite airfields.

Outside the office was a list of numbers to call for fuel. I nearly didn't call the top one, thinking they must always get the calls and might probably appreciate a break. Then I thought, what the heck, and spoke to Bill Masters. It was just as well I called because he was on his way over anyway, his wife Nancy revealed the next day.

Bill was in the Navy and then learned to fly under the GI Bill. He's one of those old-time instructors who has been there ... and survived it. At first, I thought him off-hand, but it was just his way and that of many Texans I met. Not the hollering and whooping, hard-drinking, Stetson wearing cowboys that Hollywood would have us believe.

Bill gave me a ride down to a cafeteria for dinner and and as I ate I mentioned how cheap it was to get a licence, according to the notice at Holly Springs. "I can get you a ticket in 40 hours but it takes 65 hours or more to teach you how to fly," he replied bluntly. I decided not to tell him I had set out to cross the United States with less than that in my logbook.

Next day, I heard a whistling in the air and saw Bill and a student coming in to land with the prop stationary ... a little engine-out practise introduced while the student was worrying about another thing Bill had found to switch off in flight. I asked the student afterwards what he thought about Bill. "He's a right b*****d. But if I want someone to be nice to me, I'll go pick up a girl in Dallas. If I really want to learn to fly, he's the one to teach me."

That was the kind of straight talking I had been told to expect in Texas. Tim Chesnee's business partner Al Miller splits his time between Natchez and Austin, the state capital of Texas. His favourite tale was of a tall Texan walking across the campus on his first day at Harvard when he meets a sharp-suited, fraternity-tied, senior student. "Excuse me, sir," says he, respectfully. "Could you tell me where the library's at?"

The SS, FT, SS looks him up and down as if he were something he just missed stepping in and, pointing at the Texan's chest, declares: "The first thing you must learn is that we, at Harvard, never end a sentence with a preposition."

The Texan, barely batting an eyelid, replies: "I

beg your pardon. Could you tell me where the library's at, a**hole?"

Nancy said the next day, as she was interviewing me for her weekly newspaper column on flying, that Bill had thought I had crashed into the office. He had never seen an ultralight trike parked with a wing down into the wind before.

Afterwards, when asked if the plane and pilot were alright, he muttered: "Yes, but that darn thing looked crashed the day it was built."

After a night on the office sofa, I had been ready to leave when I spotted that one of the exhaust brackets had fractured. It had been replaced just before I left, but the exhaust and radiator brackets are known to be prone to failure. Bill phoned a friend, Calvin, who took the bracket away, welded on new steel, apologised for not being able to grind it down neatly because it was a Sunday and he couldn't get the right equipment, and painted it all to look smart.

So I was back in one piece, but left waiting again for thunderstorms to pass.

"We have a way of saying things in Texas," Bill said. "You stink. There's a shower in the hangar over there and give me all your clothes and I'll wash them."

So the Flying Scotsman became the first person to use the showers in the Confederate Air Force Big Country Squadron's hangar.

The whole building is magnificent, especially when you hear that it was built by the squadron members without going into debt. There is still some work to be done inside – they haven't built the bar yet! (Is leaving it to last an incentive scheme, I wondered?) – but as Col Don "Tiny" Malm showed me around his dream project I was astounded by what they had achieved.

The next stage is to open a small museum, so even if you are just driving past, call in and see them and prepare to be inspired. They are a great bunch, and that is not just because Tiny took me 20 years back in time that afternoon with a flight in his Vultee BT13.

The Second World War trainer with its slide-back canopy is one of a handful of survivors from more than a 1,000 built. And, apart from the massive hickory stick, it brought memories flooding back of my first ever flights as a teenage cadet in Chipmunks at RAF Turnhouse, Edinburgh.

If I ever convert to three-axis control flying, it will be ideally be by being taught by Bill to fly an aircraft like this. Of course, he might not have me. Just think of all the strange control response instincts that would have to be drilled out of me.

As dusk approached, the clouds took on an amazing pattern. "Bulls balls, we call them," Bill said. "Cumulus mammatae. A sure warning of thunderstorms. You don't get them back in Scotland, do you."

Church parade was to a Southern Baptist service where Bill and Nancy worship. Three hymns, a couple of prayers, a sermon and some more singing wrapped it up. I enjoy going to church when away from home as a way of putting time aside to think of family and friends. I'm afraid the cadences of the preacher made the sermon too hard for me to follow, I think he spoke very much from the heart rather than the more intellectual approach I had been accustomed to at services in Scotland. Nancy noticed my difficulties. She quoted me in her newspaper column as saying: "I could hardly understand a word the chap said in Texas Baptist, but since I'm Scottish presbyterian I knew exactly what he was talking about."

Maybe something of the evangelical nature of the baptists rubbed off on me nonetheless, for I felt a need to crystalise the thoughts that had been building up as I flew past thunderstorms over the past few days, about how aviators have perhaps more opportunity to be in touch with God than most, maybe more need than most. We certainly have boundless opportunities and reasons for prayer. It was something to mull over once I was back in the air.

After dinner, Nancy gave me a copy of *All My Ups Have Been Downs,* a collection of short stories about her experiences around and above Texas. For British readers there is a real howler on the back cover.

"When we flew the replica Spirit of St Louis, Verne Jobst, senior pilot for United Airlines, told me the secret to being a good tailwheel pilot was to always keep my feet and fanny moving the same direction," Nancy wrote.

"I've found that philosophy work for just about every thing that happens in life."

As I had to explain to her, while in the United States fanny means a lady's behind, in Britain it means her front! Other little confusions: in the US: pattern instead of circuit; ramp instead of apron; ground instead of earth (electrics); dirt instead of ground (soil).

On Monday lunchtime, after a flight to Midland Airpark, I found a plaque at the door of the Confederate Air Force Museum hangar at Midland Regional with the following words in a tribute to the CAF's founder, Lloyd P Nolan.

"Lloyd practised no religion, save one that favoured the existence of a heaven and a God.

"Heaven, he predicted, would be a place with long runways, wide skies and an absence of turbulence. God would be a retired pilot – forgiving, inerrant, good humoured – whose role was that of a flight controller."

That summed up what I had been struggling to express after church in Abilene.

Another interesting display was about Cornelia Fort, the Tennessee aviator the Nashville airfield was named after. It noted that the mascot of the Women's Auxiliary Ferrying Squadron, of which she was a member, was called Fifinella, "a spunky little female gremlin with long eyelashes, hip boots, and gossamer wings zipping merrily out of a bank of clouds". Her job, apparently was to scare off the male gremlins who were widely known to cause aircraft malfunctions. Being superstitious, I bought a postcard of Fifinella to ward off any more broken radiator and exhaust mounts.

On the way to Midland, I flew 110 miles in a single 110 minute leg to Big Spring. An e-mail a few weeks later inquired: Why so far in one hop? Well, by now I was feeling the need to push on after problems with both an exhaust and a radiator in less than a fortnight; I was getting a tailwind across Texas, a rare treat after the Carolina headwinds; and there was the fun of flying by numbers.

In the pioneering days, Texas was divided into one square mile sections, with the boundaries running north-south and east-west. Even though many sections have since been subdivided, as far as the eye can see are parallel lines at one mile intervals running straight to the horizon.

So, to clear Abilene airspace from Elmdale, you just fly so many squares north and then so many squares west. To check groundspeed, you can count how many seconds it takes to fly across a section.

And there are not too many hills to worry about, unless you are flying a few hundred feet off the ground. It seemed to me that Texas went up in 500ft steps every 50 miles or so. The escarpments come as quite a surprise, somehow.

Big Spring is at the heart of the oilfield country, with nodding donkey wells on the airfield itself.. My only oil joke was one I told Tim in Natchez.

Q: How do you make a cat bark?

A: Pour gas on it, throw a match at it and listen for the WOOF!

I tried that with Ken Hunt at Big Spring who had earlier praised me as he refuelled the Pink Panther for doing two things no other visiting pilots do. One: calling it Big Spring singular, and not Big Springs; and two: asking where the Big Spring was.

Ken was not impressed with my joke – he keeps cats – but he still took my picture next to one of the oil wells. By the way, the Big Spring is now in a pipe under the city park.

Ken's idea of a joke was the local council building a new road on an embankment which was then washed away by some small springs. "In a town with a name like this, you'd have thought they'd have known something about the power of water," he said.

Although it had been a scorching day at Midland, I thought the air would have settled down a little by 6pm.

Wrong. Bumpy, bumpy. And not a lot of places to go. Keeping under Midland Regional's airspace gave me only 500ft to 1,000ft above the ground, and sometimes I was hitting 700ft a minute lift, and we all know that what goes up must come down, sometimes even faster. After 20 minutes I was clear of the zone and went to 1,500 ft above ground. By then the air was cooling fast, so a smooth ride to Monahans followed.

The radio, fixed at Midland Airpark, free of charge, was working and when Kermit Steria got my call he said he would hang on until I arrived to top up my tank. What service for a five gallon sale.

It had turned into another beautiful evening, so Pecos beckoned. I felt rude about making it a quick turnaround but then Angel Nabavatto arrived to enjoy the evening and rolled out his PA28-180, inviting Kermit to jump in and follow me west.

After climbing out over the masts just to the west of town, I dropped down to 200ft to follow the interstate. I came alongside two trucks and waved to the lead driver, motioning for a race. We kept neck and neck – well, after me gaining on him, he was catching up – until a bend approached and I cheated by cutting the corner. A 70mph groundspeed with a tailwind and full throttle wasn't too bad.

I then caught up with a Union Pacific freight train, flying its length before dropping down in front of the engineer's cab. I could hear the blast from his horn though my headset, I don't think he was amused.

At Pecos, Dennis Blanchard found a hangar for me to shelter the Pink Panther from the approaching storm. Dennis and his Belgian wife, Isabelle, provide a 24 hour service from their home by the airfield. Military aircraft wanting 3,000 gallons of JetAv each make his day, but he still did everything he could for a three-gallon customer. Hey, come to think of it, that amount wouldn't even fill a Texan hat, he said.

I was slow getting away in the morning. By now the area around was getting frighteningly uninhabited and I was approaching the Rockies, the historic barrier to trans-continental travel. Again, I had chosen the traditional southern route favoured by the old-timers. To the north-west was Guadalupe Peak, at 8,751ft, to the south Mt Livermore stood at 8,382ft. Of course west of the Pecos river, on the edge of the massive Edwards Plateau, I was already over 3,000ft above sea level, so the climb did not seem so daunting. Still, rather than flying straight to Van Horn, where I would begin my assault on the Rockies in earnest, I dog-legged and followed the interstate through the hills to arrive at 10:10am. Van Horn was a huge airfield and completely deserted.

Larry Simpson, commodity dealer, local newspaper publisher and editor and a few other things – no-one in this town had just one job – came out to refuel the aircraft and take me into town to pick up some breakfast. I had made the 82 miles – as the crow flies – in 105 minutes with just 3 litres of my 22 litre tank left.

Back at the airfield, I decided to try for El Paso that evening and lay on the office sofa for a snooze.

I was truly caught napping.

CRASH! A peal of thunder awoke me and a storm was about to begin. With no time to empty the machine and get the wing off it single-handed before the storm really picked up, I got the sail as best into wind as I could and then watched from the office. The wind swung round as the storm came overhead and I pulled the wing over so the other side was into wind. The only tie down was a steel chain, the ground was baked so hard I was unable to get my stakes in.

Forty minutes later, as the storm began to abate, the wind swung around again. This time, the chain snagged and before I could free the wing it was too late, the wind caught the Pink Panther and blew her onto her side. As thunderbolts crashed to the ground less than a mile away, I pulled at the undercarriage with all my strength to stop her from tumbling right over. Minutes later the sky was blue and the air calm.

The hang bracket had taken all the force. But I was not going to straighten it as Larry suggested, instead it would be a five-day wait for a new part to be flown from England. The edge of the wing had been rubbed and the fabric nose cone torn, but these could be easily patched.

My pride was another matter. In the air-conditioned dark of the motel room I lay on the bed and repeated over and over again the famous line from *Four Weddings and a Funeral*: F***, f***, f***, f***ity f***.

13

Grave Mistake

"These phantoms speak with human voices ... familiar voices, conversing and advising on my flight, discussing problems of my navigation, reassuring me, giving me messages of importance unattainable in normal life."

Charles Lindbergh

All I could think of was how careless I had been – less than 800 miles to go (maybe just a week of good flying) and here I was, stuck in a half-horse town. Van Horn is home to 3,000 people, 23 motels, 17 restaurants, seven bars (which serve wine margaritas because only private clubs get a spirits licence) and around 150 stray dogs. Needless to say, most of the local residents go to a club, so I soon became a paid-up member of the Sportsmen's Club of Van Horn.

My first few days were spent hidden away in the dark, cursing my stupidity – and laziness – at not taking the wing off for the afternoon. As I had fought to keep the Pink Panther from cartwheeling across the airfield, my only worry was that one more good gust would end my trip, piling a crumpled and shredded aircraft against the boundary fence. Now, I felt so down that I wished I had just let go of it and claimed the insurance.

I logged on to the Internet to send Greg and Todd updates on my circumstances and retrieved a stack of e-mail from people who had stumbled across my Web site. One, from Chris Bothma in South Africa was particularly heartening:

"Just surfed on in! Nice to hear from other microlighters. I'm learning to fly on a Windlass trike and three weeks ago did my first solo. INCREDIBLE!!! By the way, the weather in South Africa is great for flying. Keep up the good work."

Another came from Harry Staggs in Natchez. "Hi Colin, Sorry about your radiator problems in Natchez the other day. Read your article in the newspaper and just thought I'd write you some e-mail wishing you good luck in your flight. Must be nice to travel so freely. God speed young man."

I couldn't let down my fans. It is an old cliche, but thanks to their good wishes, my confidence began to return.

With the time difference, I had to talk to the crew at Mainair in England in the early hours of the morning, Van Horn time. Then I had to find out which freight companies served the town. The choice was between Federal Express and UPS.

The choice of places to eat was no more varied. The Old Smokehouse restaurant had a collection of vintage cars as an added attraction, Chuy's had the John Madden Haul of Fame (homage to an American sports commentator). Both sold refried beans for breakfast, lunch and dinner. Both were good of their type, but for three meals a day, for a week?

At some airfields you just get the feeling that they are bad, or unlucky, and would be as well being ploughed up. I thought it was just my own experience that made me feel that way about Van Horn until I heard of a string of tragedies over the past few years. An old man who appeared to live in a shack out by the hangar told me that in the late 1980s there had been 14 aircraft based there. But recession hit and three pilots died when their machines crashed. One was said to have been drunk at the time and overshot the mile long runway, one fell apart in mid-air and another flew into a mountain – as did a Stealth bomber, apparently.

Now there was just one aircraft, belonging to Larry and covered inches deep in bird mess, and a hang-glider in the hanger. The runways were immaculate, however, thanks to $2.5 million of federal cash spent only the year before.

The atmosphere is also a lot to do with the people running airfields. Larry seemed to be Mr Van Horn. He ran the airfield, dabbled as a commodity trader, edited and published the local newspaper, the *Van Horn Advocate*, and – as people always said – "Larry owns the local Radio Shack that his son runs". I got the feeling that he had just lost interest in flying, and the airfield atmosphere reflected that.

My days were spent writing up my diary for the Web page, sleeping during the heat of the day and telephoning friends back in Britain in the middle of the night. On the Friday night I visited the local hospital, where one of the nurses was said to have Scottish ancestry and wanted to meet her kinfolk.

Rowena, whose husband had retired from the border patrol, was a great laugh but stood for no nonsense from either patients or staff. She was just finishing her shift, so invited me back for dinner the following evening and introduced me to Dr Tillman Farley – the owner of the hang-glider.

Tillman told me he usually launched with a tow from a truck and had reached 14,000 feet in a thermal over Van Horn before coming out because he had no oxygen. He and his family also used the resurfaced runways for in-line skating.

The following evening at the hospital, my chat with Rowena and her colleague Nicole was interrupted when a prisoner from the local jail was brought in to the emergency room.

It appeared it was just a routine matter, but to my surprise he was manacled, on both hands and feet, and kept that way all through his examination and treatment. I mentioned that just before I left Britain there had been an outcry when it was discovered that pregnant prisoners were being kept chained during the birth of their children. Here, there was no sympathy for anyone who found themselves in jail. God help you if you were ever wrongly convicted, was how I felt looking at this wretched man.

A few minutes later, a woman telephoned from a motel to say her child had fallen out of its bed and could she bring it to the hospital for an examination. Rowena told Nicole to make sure and check for any signs of abuse, in case this had not been an accident.

Tillman had instructed that he was to be called to the hospital to see every patient, an order which was not popular with the nurses who felt he was only trying to soak the sick, or their insurance companies. Rowena told Nicole not to let the child's uninsured mother pay in cash, they would send out an invoice. "And I'm going to make sure it gets lost in the system," she added. I asked what the charge would have been and she said about $160. The evening was an eye opener into American medical practices. My £200 insurance policy for the three-month trip seemed a bargain.

After hearing my complaint that I had been unable to see the sights because the nearest car hire place was 80 miles away, Nicole offered to be my chauffeur. She was a single mother who had come back to Van Horn with her two young children after living in California because she could rely on her family's support during her training.

I think she enjoyed arriving at the hardware store, where her ex-husband's friends hung out, with an out-of-town stranger. There was little else to do in Van Horn other than gossip; the Community Calendar on the front page of the *Van Horn Advocate,* "The weekly newspaper serving the crossroads of scenic West Texas", had the following entries: Friday, June 7th – nothing scheduled at press time. Saturday, June 8th – nothing scheduled at press time. Sunday, June 9th – Attend the church of your choice.

The latest edition appeared just as Nicole ran me to the bus depot to pick up the spare parts from Mainair. Strangely, considering that Larry was editor and publisher, there was no mention of my trip and accident. There were no developments either on the two other big stories in town; a woman who robbed the bank and tried to make her getaway on foot with the temperature in the 90s and a man found dead in a car by the edge of the Interstate.

"I just cannot understand it," Nicole said. "Why rob a bank here in the morning, before any of the businesses have paid any money in? The woman must be crazy." Rowena and Nicole had strong views about the local police after the Interstate incident. "Can you believe those guys?" Rowena said. "That body had been in his car for two days and they called the ambulance out because they said he might still be alive. It's not a pleasant job, but if the guy's dead it's their responsibility to clear it up."

Nicole had wanted to see me fly, but she was so exhausted after a run of 12-hour shifts (that ended at 6 or 7 am and gave her just a few hours sleep before her two daughters woke her at noon) that she said she was heading straight for bed after dropping me off at the airfield.

At 7:30am it was the moment of truth. Take-off for El Paso. After a thorough pre-flight inspection I felt I might as well do the check flight tests while en route.

In the cool air, the Pink Panther leapt off the ground. A coupe of tight turns over the hospital gave me a chance to show off to the rest of the staff at the end of their shift, then I swooped down on the main street and buzzed the motel and with a wave I was back on track.

With the long shadows of dawn, I was surprised to feel a little sad at leaving Van Horn. As always, it is the people that make a place and after a few days of looking inwards at myself – and thinking what a klutz – I had begun to look around me and met some great folk.

The country around here was parched and dry. Fields where crops had once grown lay brown and abandoned. With the recession the money to pump water from wells had run dry. The storm that had caught me napping was the first rain in Van Horn for 10 months. I stuck to the Interstate for safety, that two-gallon water bottle on the cockpit floor suddenly seemed very small. Two hours later I dropped into Fabens field, about 15 miles east of El Paso and refuelled. From there, it was a short hop to West Texas, a field in uncontrolled airspace a few miles north west of El Paso.

It was a great little strip with the odd experimental aircraft passing through and a collection of relics lying around. Unfortunately, I had just missed the local EAA chapter fly-in breakfast by a day. The airfield's owner, Phil Barrett found me a spare T-hangar and I settled the Pink Panther down for the day and borrowed the airfield banger to take a run into El Paso and make a trip across the border.

As we watched a midday dust devil spiral across the end of the runway, one of the old-timers told me how a large twin-engined aircraft had been coming in the previous year when it was caught by one and slammed into the ground, destroying its undercarriage and props. It reinforced my resolution made in Van Horn to restrict my flying to the mornings.

With the delays in shipping the trike over to the States, my schedule had slipped a few weeks. Now it was getting into summer the heat in Texas was regularly hitting 100 degrees, and over in Arizona and New Mexico the mercury was nudging 120, according to the Weather Channel. The one advantage of running late was I had the benefit of the early summer tailwinds coming off the Gulf of Mexico. But this year, as I had discovered in Van Horn, the wet season with its afternoon downpours was showing signs of arriving early.

With around 700 miles to go, and a fortnight before my American visa expired, I planned to fly for a few hours in the morning, find an air-conditioned motel room to shelter from the heat in, and then be ready to go at first light the following day. Flying on again in the evening would only double my motel bills.

So now I was ready to explore El Paso. The Mexican side, Juarez, was all you have ever been warned about in a town on the wrong side of a border: cheap shops, low rent housing at high rent costs, panhandlers and swindlers. I drove for 30 minutes without stopping and then the car broke down in the queue for the US immigration control.

A few tugs on wires under the bonnet and it was working again. At the border, the US official said: "I bet you are glad to be in the States again."

The next morning I settled up with Phil, who refused to charge me for the hangar, and asked his advice for the best way west.

Phil suggested flying along the Rio Grande, the border between Mexico and the US, right though the centre of El Paso/Juarez. "The class D doesn't go into Mexico and if you keep below 500ft you will be out their way," he advised. "As long as you stay over the river, the Mexicans will think you are still in US airspace."

What he didn't tell me – and what only came into mind as I was flying along the river – was whether or not the flat ground on the Mexican bank of the river, which looked a perfect forced landing site, really was mined. The previous afternoon I had seen signs with skulls and crossbones on them along the barbed wire fence as I queued to get back to the States. Flying below the top floors of the high rise office blocks in El Paso, seeing the Pink Panther reflected in the smoked glass walls, was a stunning diversion. It was just a shame no-one was at their desks that early in the morning.

At DonaAna the sign said no fuel until 8am, so it was back in the air for Deming, but at last I was out of Texas. Thanks to Phil's advice, I abandoned the Interstate as it headed north and followed the railway. He was right in that there were places to land – a dirt track ran alongside the rails – but I wondered just how often a train went by. It would be a long walk out. To the north, the Sierra Blanca towered to 12,003ft, and all the time the ground was rising.

At West Texas there was a thermometer connected to a clockface marked in height instead of hours; the higher the mercury, the higher the indicated height. The message was, watch out for density altitude. In plain English, you need air under your wing to create lift – and the air is thinner the higher and hotter you are. Mid-morning temperatures of 100 degrees at an airfield 6,000ft above sea level decrease your rate of climb by 75 per cent and more than double your take-off distance. Extra take-off distance was no problem for the Pink Panther, except for the heating effect on tires designed to be used on wheelbarrows, but a rate of climb decreased from 1,000ft a minute at sea level in Scotland to just a couple of hundred feet a minute as I approached the Rockies was another matter. Although a previous owner of my machine had taken her to 17,000ft in Britain, he had done it in the cold, dense air of winter.

At Deming, I found a place in a hangar, chatted to a few transiting pilots and celebrated being in New Mexico. The Grand Motel was filled with pilots nightstopping: lady flier who ate what looked like an unhappy dinner alone (the next morning I heard that she had been very abrupt with the guys on the line), a couple of other general aviation types and two airborne firefighters who were taking a break from co-ordinating tankers on their run-ins to water bomb blazing forests.

The motel minibus driver didn't begin work until 7am so it was a slightly later start that I'd have liked. In the warm air, the Pink Panther seemed to eat up the runway before she broke free. Still, by 9am I was 60 miles on, in Lordsburg. On the way, in the middle of flat, scrubby desert between the rocky outcrops, was the Tarmac-coated grid pattern of an entire town – complete with street lighting, but not a single house. When I asked about it later, someone just shrugged and said a mine or something must have been planned and then cancelled at the last moment. Removing the lamp-posts would have cost more than they were worth. Memories of this unbuilt ghost town came flooding months later in Britain when I saw an advert in the *Financial Times* newspaper offering "The security of your own piece of the American West from as little as £45 ($60) per month". It must have been a different area from the parched lands I saw, for the plots in the "suburbs of fast-growing Deming, area population 20,000", were described as offering "breathtaking vistas of overlooking lush vineyards, pecan groves and sun-flooded farmland".

As I came by Lordsburg I called for and received an advisory on wind and active runway. I called out downwind leg and asked if the aircraft back-taxiing along the active runway was aware of me. No reply.

I called out my turn to base.

As I was turning on to final, the aircraft radioed that it was taxiing onto the runway for take-off.

"There's an aircraft on final if you look out the window," I transmitted.

"Okay," came the reply.

To save taxiing down a mile of runway, I kept my height at 250ft as I went over the numbers and planned to land near the FBO at the far end.

"Are you landing or aren't you?" came the next transmission.

"Just landing very long to get out of your way as soon as possible," I replied. And thought the further out of your way the better.

It turned out he was a local chap who had only turned his radio on just before take-off "because it is normally a very quiet airfield".

The wind looked like it was picking up, so I unloaded the Pink Panther, took the wing off and tucked it in the hangar. Only when the wing is off and laid on a hangar floor do people really begin to appreciate just how big it is. As army and border patrol choppers flew in to this "quiet" airfield, I was glad my wing was well sheltered.

I got talking to one of the people hanging around the office and asked if he wanted to join me for lunch. David Thomas was hauling water for a firm digging a pipeline trench across the desert, but some equipment had broken down so there was nothing to do for the day (and no pay for him either). So, as a pilot, he had wandered down to the airfield to see what was going on.

Over lunch, he told me he had been a salesman and used his aircraft to fly around and meet his customers. He was mildly dyslexic and his wife had helped him write reports, but when he got promoted to a manager things just got too much. Now he was a member of the Teamsters union and worked away from home for six months of the year, saving up his pay so he could enjoy the other half of the year with his family.

After lunch at AJ's cafe – whose motto is Mark Twain's witticism: "Part of the secret of success in life is to eat what you like and let the food fight it out inside" – David said: "Hey, we found some really unusual graves out where we are working. Do you want to come on a trip out in the desert to see them?" Well, why not?

We had been driving along a dirt track for about 10 minutes when David pulled to a halt. All around, the ground was arid, featureless scrub, not a grave in sight. I was about to say something when he opened the glovebox and pulled out a revolver.

"Oh no. How am I going to explain this to my parents if there really is a heaven where we'll all meet up," I thought. "All that love and dedication snuffed out in an instant because I went off into the desert with a complete stranger. A stranger who invited me to look at a grave."

"I saw a tin can over there, feel like some plinking," David said.

Holding the revolver with my arm straight, quite an achievement considering the adrenaline flowing through my body, I got two hits from six shots. Not bad for the first time with a handgun. From the hip, cowboy style, I managed another two hits. David was sure I was an old hand.

The graves were next to the railroad track, each marked with an oval of stones and crosses made from what appeared to be driftwood. One looked child sized, the other two were almost the same size each. It looked like a family plot.

Down the tracks at Steins railroad ghost town, everyone knew of the graves but no-one knew the story. Many thought, for no apparent reason, it may have been a Chinese family working on the railroad. But others suggested that it was a pioneering family killed by Indians. New Mexico was a federal territory until earlier this century because it simply didn't have a large enough population to be a state, so there aren't too many oldtimers about to help with history.

In the shade of the porch in front of the general store, Larry Link told me how Steins had been built at the top of the pass through the mountains as a staging post for the early wagon trails. Unfortunately, there was no natural water source, so water hauled from Doubtful Canyon sold for a dollar a barrel.

"One of your journalistic predecessors, a reporter from the New York Herald, passed through here around 1860 and thus tales of the Wild West began," Larry said.

"And most of them were true, not like what you read in them newspapers today. In April 1861, five men travelling west by stagecoach to Tucson were attacked by Cochise and his band while approaching here. Two were killed in the first exchange of fire. They were the lucky ones.

"The others survived long enough to be hung upside down and burned alive."

When the Southern Pacific built a railroad through the pass, Steins' future seemed assured with the railway hauling train-loads of water there to supply the steam locomotives. But when the company switched from steam to diesel, there was no need to haul water any more and the town, which had a population of 1,300 at its peak between 1903 and 1945, died overnight.

Larry said that it was also a favourite spot for robberies, because the trains were travelling so slowly at the top of the pass. One raider, Thomas E "Black Jack" Ketchum , was captured in 1901 after being shot in the arm. By the time he was caught, the wound had turned gangrenous and his arm had to be amputated.

Once he had recovered he was hung for his crimes. The eight-foot drop ripped his head off and he was the last man hanged in New Mexico.

As David and I looked around the collection of crumbling walls and dusty buildings, one of the massive freight trains went by. By the time the locomotives were out of sight, I still could not see the end of it. Each train was 10,000ft long – that's more than two miles.

Back in the air next morning, I tracked down David's truck and put on a display of stalls and tight turns before overflying Steins en route to Cochise County airfield at Willcox. The air coming though the pass made it too bumpy for many photographs – the few I took came out blurred. But the tales Larry told of a town with more bordellos than saloons helped paint vivid pictures of life in the Old West in my mind as I followed the Interstate. And I had made it over the Rockies – although the summit of Mt Graham to the north of me was at 10,713ft, from here it was downhill all the way to California's Salton Sea.

As I came out on to the plain, there was a bizarre zig-zag line defining the border, with green fields in Mexico and dusty brown ones in the States. It is not that the Mexicans get all the rain, it's that they get all the work. Rather than grow crops, the American farmers just sell their water across the border.

Approaching Willcox, a thunderstorm cell was firing off lightening bolts a few miles to the south west. So although it was just 8:15am Lordsburg time (7:15am mountain time), I decided to get the machine safely under cover. Seventy one miles was better than nothing.

A couple of other aircraft heading west arrived, including an AirCoupe that had heard about me that morning at Lordsburg. As the cell dissipated, I called flight service for an update, but they reported a huge amount of thermic activity over Tucson, 90 miles away.

"It will have cleared up by the time I get there," I told myself. "No, remember what happened in Van Horn – where will you go if Tucson is surrounded by thunderstorms, it's also surrounded my 8,000ft mountains?" another voice said.

Caution got the upper hand, we all decided to wait. An hour later, it was all clear along the route. But it was too late for me. An hour or two down the line it would be getting too thermic and bumpy for an easy day.

"I should have left an hour ago," I thought. "I knew the storms would clear up." Of course I hadn't. It had been wishful thinking, the sort that more often than not gets you into trouble.

14

Final Frontier

Oh I have slipped the surly bonds of Earth
And danced the skies on laughter-silvered wings
Sunward I've climbed, and joined the tumbling mirth
Of sun-split clouds —and done a hundred things
You have not dreamed of — wheeled and soared
and swung, High in the sunlit silence.

Fl Lt John Gillespie Magee Jn, from his poem *High Flight*

P
rudence has its reward, they say, and mine that day was the use of a fabulous pre-oil crisis 1972 Ford in a wonderful blend of verdigris green and rust red for a trip to the Chiricahua national monument where the Indian leader Cochise once had one of his many strongholds. In a spooky co-incidence, one ridge even looks like the silhouette of an Indian warrior's head.

Picking up fuel at Willcox I got the impression that the aircraft in just before me had woken up Louise, who runs the field with her husband Jim. He is a late riser, she said, who ends up working on aircraft in the heat of the afternoon instead of taking a siesta, so he was happy late that afternoon to share a cold Coke with me and discuss a route.

His advice was to head north west, up the San Pedro river valley to the west of the Galiuro Mountains and around the back of the 9,157ft Mt Lemmon. There were many forced landing sites all along the river and farmhouses where one could seek help, and the route would take me away from the crowded airspace around Tucson. With far fewer airfields around, the route planning gave me plenty to think about for the evening.

The sheer contrast the next morning between the lush green fields next to the river – which was only a trickle of water – and the parched mountain sides was a stark reminder of how harsh the local environment really is, and a testament to the strength of those pioneers who settled here. It is hard to grasp just how little they must have known about the area and just how desperate the conditions were that they had left behind to start a new life in unknown and unfriendly territory.

At San Manual I made a quick stop to change fuel tanks and stretch my legs before swinging around to the west again. The town was dominated by a massive mining complex and there seemed to be a popular little flying club at the airfield. A couple of people took my picture before wishing me good fortune.

Over the hills to the valley north of Tucson I passed Biosphere II, an attempt to create a self-sustaining garden of Eden. This "planet in a bottle" was designed to be a self-sustaining eco-system replicating the Earth – Biosphere I – with rain forest, sea, marsh, desert and savannah under a three-acre glass and steel greenhouse. In 1991, eight people were sealed in as part of the experiment, but within 18 months the oxygen levels had fallen to that found at 17,000ft and it became overrun by crazy ants and morning glories. I was several thousand feet up to get clear of the worst of the thermals, but decided to dive down and give it a buzz to add to the chaos.

By now, the air was getting busy, with aeroplanes in sight every few minutes, mostly heading up and down Interstate 10 between Tucson and Phoenix. This was the greatest amount of traffic I had seen, so far.

Pinal Airpark, just across the Interstate, was a must on two counts. One, it is an aircraft boneyard for unwanted civil jets. Two, it was said to be the home base for the modern day CIA equivalent of Air America.

I transmitted the usual calls on joining downwind, turning base, and finally announced I was set up for a short final. Then I heard someone saying they were on long finals five miles to the north. "Aircraft calling long final for Pinal, this is ultralight G-MWXU on short final, please identify yourself," I transmitted. "Ultralight, we have visual on you. Be advised we are a C-47 inbound about four miles from Pinal."

These four-engined guys were not doing a go-around. They landed so close behind I thought their prop wash was going to catch me as I zipped off onto a taxiway.

The tales of it being a CIA base seemed true enough when, as soon as I halted on the ramp, a jeep pulled up with two paramiltary dressed men in it closely followed by truck with a security guard. The men just wanted to know what sort of aircraft the Pink Panther was, where I was flying to and from and how fast I cruised – the usual airfield chat.

After they drove off, the guard asked if I knew them. When I replied no, he told me I was not authorised to speak to anyone on the field except in connection with refuelling and warned me not to stray towards any of the hangars.

Well, I cannot say I uncovered any secrets. I must have, however, spoken to just about everyone on the field because pilots and ground crew were drawn to the Pink Panther like flies to honey – until I asked if I could take a photograph with the jets in the background. Quicker than you could say cheese, they all vanished.

A letter from my parents perhaps revealed the true reason for their interest, I thought. According to the *Daily Mail* of 29 May, the RAF were considering trikes for strikes at Saddam in the Gulf because they could operate from rough ground and were almost invisible to radar. The illustration showed a microlight almost identical to mine equipped with a Maverick missile slung under the fuselage and a pilot wearing night vision goggles. And the story claimed that with the same Rotax 582 engine that powered the Pink Panther it would fly at 130mph. Needless to say, it was completely untrue. Air traffic control radar, for instance, had no problem seeing my trike on their screens when I was more than 30 miles away from the airfield.

From Pinal, it was up the Interstate to Casa Grande. Boy, things were getting busy with traffic everywhere. I was glad I had taken the scenic route to the northeast of Tucson.

At Casa Grande, the wind appeared to favour an approach from the east but there was no reply to a request for an airfield advisory.

I then saw another aircraft taxiing along to the end of runway zero-six. I checked the wind, looking at dust trails behind cars, etc and determined that two-four was the best runway for me and called out I was on downwind. As I turned onto base, the aircraft on the ground was going through its pre-take-off checks and had not acknowledged any of my transmissions.

I knew my radio had been working just a few minutes earlier when passing over another airfield where parachutists were jumping because I had been in communication with the jump plane. But as

I called out I was on finals, the Casa Grande aircraft taxied onto the end of the runway, announced it was taking off and started its run.

"Aircraft taking off on zero-six at Casa Grande, ultralight is on finals for two-four. Can you see me?" I transmitted.

There was no reply, so: "Ultralight on finals at Casa Grande is going around for a left-hand pattern, two-four Casa Grande."

I suppose I should have climbed out to the right, but then I would have been in a right-hand pattern. Anyway, as soon as the Cessna was off the ground I swung round and plopped down on runway two-four well before it could have come back round for another landing.

On the ground, I found I was the one who had landed the right way. Yes, this was another woman pilot taking off downwind – just like at Palatka. But this time I had stuck to my own observations and landed into wind.

There was no sign of anyone at the field for fuel so I changed tanks and thought: "Let's get out of here, this could be another of these strange, unhappy airfields."

As I taxied out, another aircraft was seeking a traffic advisory. The woman Cessna pilot was just taking off – downwind – for another circuit but never acknowledged the transmission. I replied: "Winds favour two-four. Cessna in pattern flying downwind landing and take-offs. Ultralight taxiing for take-off downwind on zero-six to avoid conflict. Recommend overflight to check out situation. Cessna seems unable to receive radio transmissions."

I later heard the incoming Piper calling out he was landing on two-four, so if I was wrong I was not the only one! An instructor once told me the basic rule of flying is that the wind goes in the big end of a windsock and comes out the little end. Once that is sorted out, everything else is easy. Maybe they teach things a different way in America.

The 54 miles to Gila Bend were nerve wracking. It was getting late in the morning and rather than going north to pick up the Interstate, I took the direct route over some fairly rugged and bleak terrain. At least I knew my radio was working in case of an emergency. As the minutes went by, the ground became more and more corrugated, then it became boulder-strewn. I began to regret not taking the longer way round, but by now it was as far to the road as it was to Gila Bend.

As the ground finally began to fall away, I kept my height and six miles out from the airfield I was 5,000ft above the ground, reluctant to drop down too soon and enter the thermals. It was 105 degrees on the surface, and when I got to 2,000 ft above the airfield the hot wind just blasted me as though I was in front of a giant hairdrier. There was no cooling effect at all from the 70 mph breeze as I dived off height.

An empty airfield, but efficient service. I was glad I had made the effort to reach it that day when I discovered it was closed on Sundays. A stop at Casa Grande would have seen me stranded for a day without fuel, for my next leg was to Yuma, at 102 miles my longest planned single flight so far. It was also going to be my first into an airfield with an active control tower.

After lunch I settled in to my air-conditioned room at the Yucca Motel to go over my route and watch television. With a mid-afternoon temperature of 120 degrees, it was too hot to use the motel pool.

My aim, as always, was a dawn take-off. But as the sun burst over the horizon, the rose-coloured glow on the mountains made the perfect backdrop for the Pink Panther and a giant cactus. It was the photograph I had dreamt off during those late nights on the newspaper in Edinburgh.

Even though the FBO was closed for the day, my radio procedure was immaculate. I had been told off the previous day for mispronouncing the name, I should have said Hee-la Bend. The two-hour flight along the Interstate, between two restricted military areas paved with abandoned Second World War airfields, was uneventful. Now

I was just clocking up the miles, desperate to reach the coast. Life inland was just too hot without air-conditioning, so the atmosphere in these small towns – Gila Bend had an official population of just 1,747 – at this time of year was one of dull survival, a dash from air-conditioned homes to air-conditioned cars to air-conditioned shops to air-conditioned offices and back again. Except I didn't have air-conditioning, so felt left out. I wondered what those wartime bomber crews felt like when they arrived in Europe after training in the desert.

Just east of Yuma I had to climb a few thousand feet to get over some mountains. My radio worked fine, the tower was now open and I got clearance for a straight-in approach from five miles out. The only thing is, that was a seven or eight minute final for me. I tried explaining this, but every couple of minutes the tower would ask me where I was. Fortunately, I could hear no other traffic so I guess I did not get in anyone's way.

But that was the landing. On take-off half an hour later after refuelling, just as ground control left me holding for runway one-seven and told me to switch to the tower, my radio died!

What was I to do? I had no way to let the tower know my intentions and both the east-west and north-south runways, which intersect, were being used by commercial passenger carriers. I also could not contact ground control for taxiing clearance.

Even if I had had flares or flashing lights, I couldn't remember what the codes were. Eventually I realised the short taxiway back to the FBO did not cross a runway, so I turned back and then telephoned the tower to let them know what had happened.

The little box of tricks that switches between my regulator, headsets, radio and press-to-talk switch had played up again and the radio battery had gone flat. So after 45 minutes on charge and a strong coffee I reckoned I had enough power to get me off the ground and out of the controlled airspace.

I was just about right. Yuma is at the end of a pointed piece of Mexico that sticks up into the United States at the border of California and Arizona. A hill right on the point makes an excellent marker for the frontier and the edge of the Yuma zone. I reported to the tower I was passing to the north of it and then the radio started to go again as I picked up the Interstate. What could I do, I was out of the zone, so a radio wasn't essential, I thought. I certainly couldn't turn back and there wasn't anywhere to land that looked as though it might have a telephone.

A few minutes later I saw a biplane coming up behind me. I waved at him and he threw himself into a tight turn and headed back east. I then realised he had probably been asked by the Yuma tower to check I was still in the air, if not on the air.

Imperial County field at El Centro was a breeze to find on the flat plain running ahead of me to the far mountains, which were now being obscured by haze.

On landing, the altimeter read minus 56 feet, my first touchdown below sea level. (Although some would say that some of my landings have been so heavy I must have thought the runway was another few hundred feet lower. About that bump: it's not my fault, it's not the plane's fault, it's the asphalt!)

After fuelling up I asked about hangar space. There seemed to be a few empty bays, so when I was told they were all full I asked if there was one belonging to someone away for the weekend that I could use.

No dice. The only space was a tie-down on the ramp, not even a nice dirt patch behind a hangar to screw my stakes into. So I unloaded the Pink Panther, took off the wing and tied the nose to the trike keel under the engine. The rest of the wing I weighted down with fuel tanks.

That night I could hardly sleep. Once over the mountains my trip would be complete. Coast-to-coast, solo – apart from a few hops where I had given Gerry and James a lift – in a flex-wing. At first, it had seemed too far away to be possible. Then I began to suffer problem after problem. Now the coast was just a two-hour hop over the hills.

I studied the map and studied it again. I programmed the GPS and radio, ordered pizza and watched *Top Gun* on the movie channel.

The huge difference in weather conditions on either side of the mountains gave me a headache. Dawn was at 6am, and a flight then would avoid the heat and thermals. But on the other side there was the "June gloom", the morning sea fog that could envelop the coast until after lunchtime. I decided on an 8am start to get over the mountains before it got too hot and windy and yet not arrive on the other side before the morning fog had lifted. By heading for Ramona, 1,500ft above the coast, I could get over the mountains and then wait for an hour until the sea fog had cleared, if need be.

But disaster struck again. Down on the ramp, the wing lay almost 180 degrees round from where I had left it the previous night. It was still the right way up, still tied to the trike, but had two gashes in the sailcloth where it seemed the bottom two blades of the prop had punctured it.

I still have not worked out what happened. The best theory is that a helicopter landed in the night and the fabric billowed up, was caught by the prop and swung the trike right round.

So, instead of a flight to the beach it was a trip to Walmart for a needle and thread. The gashes sewn up, I then glued a patch over them and sewed around the edges, finishing off with a special glue to stop the thread unravelling.

All this in 100 degree-plus heat with no shade and by a person who had never successfully sewn on a button before.

The next morning, it flew fine. And with the radio fully recharged I got clearance for a 1,500 ft overhead transit of the nearby El Centro airforce base. The Blue Arrow aerobatic team is based there, but there was just one aircraft on the ramp. I asked permission to cut the corner of a restricted zone to the north, but was told by the airforce tower I should be talking to Edwards AFB. I didn't bother. Who needed the hassle? Once over the airfield I hugged the ground and took the longer route for a low-level flight out of the wind to the foothills of the San Pasqual mountains and the climb to get over the pass, my final frontier.

At 6,000ft this was quite high by itself, but fearful of mountain wave and rotor at the summit as the hot desert air clashed with the cool sea breeze, I decided to keep climbing and stay in smooth air. And then I thought: "We're not allowed over 10,000ft back home without oxygen, this is my chance to set a new personal high."

So I reached 10,200ft at the top, took a picture of the altimeter with the smog/fog bound coast ahead, and began my descent into Ramona. It was interesting beginning to feel some very mild effects of hypoxia: drowsiness, lack of energy, euphoria, cold. Of course it *was* cold two miles up and wearing just shorts and a tee-shirt under my Goretex suit. And I did feel euphoric, my destination was in sight!

The climb had burnt almost a full tank of fuel so a mid-air change was in order, with that few minutes of worry until you are sure it is the new tank you are running on and not just the last drops of fuel in the lines. But nothing could stop me now. The coast was about 12 miles away, I was more than two miles up and I had a glide angle of at least eight to one. Whatever happened, I would reach the beach.

At Ramona, the forecast was hazy but clear right down to the coast so I refuelled and took off for Oceanside. A great name for an airfield to end the trip, I thought. I should have remembered the snow at Hot Springs.

I would be wrong if I said I was unwelcome at Oceanside, although during the ultralight craze of the 1980s the county passed laws banning ultralights after people started taking off from the street outside their homes. Fortunately, with my British registration and pilot's licence, I was able to claim regular aircraft status and escape prosecution!

There was no hangarage there and I wanted to reward myself with a day or two at the beach, so the airfield manager suggested telephoning Palomar, seven miles down the coast.

Cinema Air had hangar space, at $20 a night, but I reckoned that the Pink Panther had earned it.

I telephoned the tower to let them know I was coming, had hangarage booked and asked if there was a quiet period I could arrive in because I my airspeed was just 50 miles an hour airspeed. "No problem, come anytime. This afternoon's fine. Just call us on the radio once you are off the ground at Oceanside," I was told.

I took off due west down the river to the beach at Oceanside and out over the Pacific. My destination at last.

Palomar asked me to squawk a code on my transponder.

"Palomar tower, that is a negative. Golf Mike Whisky X-ray Uniform has no transponder or electrical system," I replied.

"Ultralight Whisky X-ray Uniform have you a transponder exemption from San Diego?"

"Palomar. That is a negative. I do not need one. Repeat, I have no electrical system. The radio and GPS are battery operated."

"Oh?"

"Affirmative, Palomar. Please check your FARs (federal airworthiness regulations) and confirm."

"Standby, ultralight."

For a couple of minutes there was silence. Then:

"Ultralight, please call when downwind opposite the tower."

After that, I would like to say I made a triumphant arrival. However, as I was about to touch down a gust of wind caught me and I ballooned about ten feet before catching it and making a firm, although not too heavy landing.

It was not the smooth, show off, float-in finale that I had planned.

That night in the Village Pub in Carlsbad, the resort by the beach, I met a sports reporter from the *North County Times*. When the barman told him what I was celebrating, he set up an interview with a colleague, Terry Wells, the following morning.

Terry asked the obvious question: "Is this a first?"

"Well, I don't know," I replied. "I know two men from England who flew across the States in a flex-wing trike, taking turns to fly the aircraft and drive their back-up truck. So I suppose they only flew half-way each. And there's a German couple who did something similar who I heard about in Crossville, Tennessee.

"But as far as I know I'm the first to fly solo against the prevailing wind across the USA from east to west in a trike – and may be the first solo crossing in a trike either way."

Whatever, I flew 2,794 miles in 69 hours and 50 minutes from Kitty Hawk, North Carolina, to

Palomar, California. That makes for an average groundspeed of 40mph.

I wrecked a hang bracket, stressed a Jesus bolt, ripped the wing fabric and slightly bent a couple of other bits. Three times during my trip I thought I was minutes from death, although only one of those was in the air. Cal Rodgers, on the other hand, crashed 19 times on the first trans-continental flight and arrived in California from New York with only a wing strut and a rudder of his original aircraft, a Wright Model B, intact. But Cal's was a pioneering flight, mine simply a grand adventure.

A fortnight later, as I sat on the jumbo jet from LA to New York, I was wondering what Cal would have thought of this massive machine, and my rag-tag trike, when the fasten seatbelts sign came on as we hit turbulence over the Rockies. While my fellow passengers did their best not to look nervous, I flicked through the in-flight magazine and gazed at the world map, with flying times marked between the major cities. A whole continent covered in hours, not months.

I looked at Russia. Now how far is it across there? And if I set off from East Fortune I would have a tailwind, I might get 60mph...

YORK HOUSE, EDINBURGH